Praise for

Magic Words

"The human ability to use words allows us to communicate
with others, to communicate with ourselves (which is to
think), and, finally, to acquire the attitudes by which we per-
ceive the world. *Magic Words* embraces all three. It helps us
communicate more effectively, more persuasively with others; it helps us think more clearly and more positively, even
like ourselves better. Most important is its hidden force: it
affects our attitudes, how we see people and situations, in a
most joyful way. This book is a delightful celebration of who
can be at our best. So here are two *Magic Words* for my
friends Howard Kaminsky and Alexandra Penney: Thank
you."   —Walter Anderson, Chairman and Publisher, *Parade*

"Thank you, Howard and Alexandra, for showing grown-ups
how to master our manners, rule our reactions, and, of
course, nicely conquer the world."

—Diane Sawyer, ABC News

"*Magic Words* by Howard Kaminsky and Alexandra Penney
should save a lot of relationships. I suggest that every day
you should stand in front of the mirror, and after combing
your hair and brushing your teeth, you should recite some
magic words. What a great idea!"   —Dr. Ruth Westheimer

"I loved *Magic Words*. I take it with me everywhere, and steal
its best quotes without shame."   —Mel Brooks

"Somehow magic words can ease a hurt, quell a skirmish, and just make people feel a lot better in a couple of seconds. This delightful book is broken into short chapters—actually 101 of them—on the simple words that can guide you through life's challenges." —Carol Fitzgerald, *bookreporter.com*

"A little powerhouse of a book . . . [It] makes life's little stumbling blocks more bearable by providing you with "magic words"—phrases you can say like mantras to guide you through tough times . . . So get off the fence, go after your dreams, and take your place at life's banquet table. It's a new year." —*Bookpage*

"These magic words compress human wisdom and experience into assimilible bites . . . eminently readable and fun to ponder." —San José Public Library Readers' Connection

Magic Words

Magic Words

101 WAYS TO TALK YOUR WAY THROUGH LIFE'S CHALLENGES

Howard Kaminsky
& Alexandra Penney

BROADWAY BOOKS | NEW YORK

A hardcover edition of this book was published in 2002
by Broadway Books.

PRINTED IN THE UNITED STATES OF AMERICA

BROADWAY BOOKS and its logo, a letter B bisected on the diagonal, are
trademarks of Random House, Inc.

Visit our website at www.broadwaybooks.com

First trade paperback edition published 2004

Book design by Gretchen Achilles

The Library of Congress has cataloged the hardcover edition as follows:
Kaminsky, Howard.
Magic words: 101 ways to talk your way through life's challenges / by
Howard Kaminsky and Alexandra Penney.—1st ed.
p. cm.
1. Interpersonal communication. 2. Interpersonal relations. 3. Social
psychology. 4. Life skills. I. Penney, Alexandra. II. Title.
HM1166 K35 2001
302—dc21   2001035664

ISBN 0-7679-0669-1

1 3 5 7 9 10 8 6 4 2

THIS BOOK IS FOR OUR MAGICAL FAMILY: SUSAN, JESSICA, DENNIS, JOHN, JULIE, ERIN, PAUL.

AND, OF COURSE, FOR ALL OUR MAGICAL FRIENDS WHO SHARE OUR FAVORITE MAGIC WORDS, "LET'S GRAB SOME RIBS AND SEE A MOVIE."

CONTENTS

Introduction   xv

Magic Words
YOU SAY TO YOURSELF

1.	Can I Say "I Love You" Too Much?	3
2.	It's Thimble Time	6
3.	It's Body Armor Time	9
4.	Volta Mind Control	12
5.	KMS	15
6.	The Best Offense Is More Offense	17
7.	Let It Go	20
8.	It's Only Me	22
9.	Sitting on the Fence Is Fine for My Cat	24
10.	Stress Level No. 5	27
11.	I'll Sing for My Supper, but I Won't Audition	30
12.	When You Draw the Line, Do It in Cement	33
13.	Playing Fast and Loose Is Fine on the Football Field	37
14.	Why Am I Smiling When I Feel Angry as Hell?	39

15. Anyone Can Screw Me Once
    (I Said Once!)   41
16. I'll Take the Next Flight Out   44
17. I Don't Think I Want You in My Lifeboat   48
18. I Only Need One   51
19. Mope or Cope? It's Really an Easy Call   54
20. There Are Better Things to Take a Chance
    on Than Lottery Tickets   57
21. Hold On! I Think I'm Ready to Lighten Up:
    #1—The Folks   59
22. Hold On! I Think I'm Ready to Lighten Up:
    #2—The Ex-Spouse   62
23. Hold On! I Think I'm Ready to Lighten Up:
    #3—The Sibling(s)   64
24. Hold On! I Think I'm Ready to Tighten Up:
    #1—The Boss   67
25. Hold On! I Think I'm Ready to Tighten Up:
    #2—The Friends   70
26. Hold On! I Think I'm Ready to Tighten Up:
    #3—The Kids   73
27. Share Your Fears with Yourself and Your
    Courage with Others   76
28. Clarity Tomorrow (or the Next Day)   78
29. Of All the Many Voices, Listen to the
    Nearest One—Yours   82
30. Get Your Ego Out of It!   84
31. If I Don't Start, I Don't Have a Problem   87
32. When Is Saying "I'm Sorry" Not Enough?   90
33. I'm Going to Lend Myself a Helping
    Hand   92
34. Wind It, Don't Turn It Back   95
35. "I-Need"s   98

36. If You Want to Gain Control, You Have to
    Give Up Control   100
37. Hey, It's Only the Second Inning   102
38. If Lions Are Such Messy Eaters, Why Do
    I Always Want the Lion's Share?   104
39. I'm Not Lonely When I'm Alone   106
40. Keep in Motion (or K.I.M.)   108
41. I Have to Stop Grieving for You Now (But I'm
    Never Going to Stop Loving You)   111
42. Futurista   114
43. The Gift of Worry   116
44. Think, Don't Feel   119
45. Don't Punt on the First Down   122
46. Ask It   125
47. Step Back to Get Closer   128
48. So, [Your Name Goes Here], Why Are You
    Buying This?   131
49. Mirror, Mirror, Who the Hell Am I?   134

Magic Words ·
YOU SAY TO OTHERS

50. This Stress Belongs to You   139
51. Are You Actually Yelling at Me?   142
52. Whiskers   144
53. I've Decided Not to Decide   147
54. Let's Quit While We're Behind   150
55. Why Are You Asking?   153
56. How About Letting Me Be a Pillow of Strength?   155
57. This Is a Pewter Opportunity   158
58. Let's Read the Writing on the Wall   161
59. Let Me Think About It   163

60. Please, Don't Be So Rude   165

61. A Stiff Upper Lip Should Tremble Now and Then   168

62. I Want to Give You Another Shot   171

63. Let's Have a Bad Time   175

64. I'm Mystified   178

65. Even a Frisbee Takes Sides   180

66. You Can't Try Again Until You Hang Up   183

67. An Old Broom Generally Sweeps as Well
    as a New One   185

68. It's Not the Cure for Cancer   188

69. Can You Save It?   192

70. Now or Never? Give Us a Break!   195

71. It's a Rough Patch in the Long Road of Life   197

72. I Need Your Help   200

73. Washing Dirty Linen Should Only Be Done
    in the Laundromat   203

74. How Can We Split Up If We Haven't Even
    Started Yet?   205

75. What Do You Know That I Don't Know?   208

76. That's More Than I Care to Know   210

77. My Being on Time Really Requires Your Help   212

78. Hey! You're Standing on My Foot   215

79. A Few Good Friends Make You Very Popular   218

80. Don't Forget You're NOT in a Telephone Booth!   221

81. I Like to Dance, but Can't We Take Turns Leading? 223

Magic Words
UNIVERSAL

82. Handle with Flair   229

83. You Can't Run the Race Unless You See
    the Finish Line   231

84. Look Closely at the First Syllable of CONfidence 234
85. The 60 Percent Solution 236
86. There Are Some Boxes You Should Just
    Not Open 238
87. Viagra, Unlike Niagara (Falls, That Is), Is a
    Two-Way Proposition 240
88. 300-Second Sex 243
89. A Fact in Time Saves More Than Nine 245
90. Praise Is a Short Word That Goes a Long Way 247
91. There's Only One Condition for Friendship 249
92. Not Every Improvement Is a Meaningful
    Improvement 252
93. If You Weren't There, You Really Weren't There 255
94. The Devil Does Rentals 258
95. Anger Is One Letter Short of Danger 261
96. When You Get into a Downward Spiral, Hit the
    Ground Running 263
97. Public Enemy #2 266
98. Ego Snacks 269
99. The Clean Slate Club 272
100. Connect-Connect 275
101. Time Is Honey 277

Afterword 281

INTRODUCTION

Magic Words are not new. We were all given some when we were kids. The first one was "please." Then came "thank you" and "excuse me." They were followed by "may I?" and "you're welcome." We still use those and they work just fine.

Those particular Magic Words gave us the manners we needed to deal with the outside world. Others we were taught had a different purpose: they were only for the family, reminders meant to remain invisible to the rest of the world. In our families, our mothers used "Family Hold Back," spoken aloud as "FHB," as a warning that the food at a party was running low and family members were to pass up second helpings. That one became so common among our generation that the last time we heard it at a dinner party, half the guests at the table immediately looked guilt stricken and conscientiously refused seconds.

Of those Magic Words that provided information while keeping the situation invisible to outsiders, one of our favorites was uttered by a family matriarch at a dinner party in a harborside restaurant in Maine. The woman eyed her husband and announced firmly, "Isaiah 6:5," whereupon the elderly gentleman hastily left the room. Naturally we asked what that was about, and the daughter of the clan filled us in. Her mother had noticed that her father's fly was unzipped. In family parlance, the reference was a witty warning from the Bible: "Woe is me! For I am undone."

The Magic Words in this book are as useful as the ones we learned in childhood—although they focus on problems we didn't face when we were kids. Some help us deal with the rest of the world. Others are for private consumption, reminders to ourselves of how we should behave or react in difficult situations. They cover a wide range of problems and, like the Magic Words of childhood, they work. You might call them "101 Magic Words for People over Twelve."

Let's start off by telling you a little about ourselves and where *Magic Words* came from. We've been friends a long time—over twenty years. More than good friends. "Family close." Oddly, there have been no fights, no major disagreements. Sure, we've each thought the other to be a little crazy at times, but we've always understood that everyone *needs* to be a little crazy once in a while. Over the years, we've counseled each other during rough times: broken hearts, splintered jobs, family health problems, major decisions about where to live or how to live. We've made friends together, shared and embraced each other's friends—in other words, we've lived through the usual ups and downs, twists and turns, some a bit hair-raising, that we all call life.

During our decades of friendship we've always been there for each other. When things have been pretty rough for either of us, or for our friends or families, we've made it a habit to meet for a drink or a Chinese dinner. Over cold vodkas one July night years ago, we were discussing a very close mutual friend who was having a tough time. The mainstays of Sue's life—marriage, career, family—were all suddenly at a critical juncture.

Alexandra, who had just spoken to Sue, said, "She feels she's in a downward spiral, spinning toward disaster."

"I know what that's like," said Howard, "and, yeah, everything could crash, but anytime you're in a downward spiral you have to get ready to hit the ground running. She can't just freeze, thinking about the things that might happen. She's got to get ready to cope if they do."

"'If you're in a downward spiral, hit the ground running,'" said Alexandra. "You said that to me once, and it changed the way I handled things. They were Magic Words. Instead of lying awake worrying about some terrible thing happening, I sat down and worked out what I'd do."

That night we both realized we'd been using Magic Words with each other for as long as we could remember. And we understood that they had enormous power. They made us see things in a different light, made us able to cope with overwhelming predicaments, gave us simple, practical, useful ways of looking at ourselves and dealing with the stressful and sometimes traumatic times that all of us face as we navigate our lives.

"Think of some of our other Magic Words," Alexandra prodded. She took out some scraps of paper and a pen, and we began making a list. Many of the words we remembered were learned from teachers, parents, and mentors. Others came from help and advice we'd given to each other, to other friends, or to family members facing difficult situations at home or at the office. Over the years, we added to our list in a casual way. Whenever either of us repeated a phrase that had transformative potential—that had power and punch—we would write it down. Our Magic Words became mantras for us. "Time is honey" was a reminder that you need sweetness in your life as well as work. The softly spoken words "Are you actually yelling at me?" could cut off a screamer's escalating anger. "Mope or cope" was a call to get up off the couch and do something about a problem. "Public enemy #2" was a warning about the monster Envy. We used our Magic Words all the time. Sometimes we repeated them to ourselves, sometimes to others who needed them. When the list began getting long and unwieldy, we divided the Magic Words into two categories.

"Magic Words You Say to Yourself" are mantras, reminders, or triggers. If you find yourself in a difficult place, surrounded by clouds of fear, anxiety, loneliness, and stress, the Magic Words can help. They're pungent, effective phrases that can protect you in emotional storms. They can also motivate you to communicate more clearly, to stick with a diet, to lighten up—or, as we say, to "tighten up." They can help you to know yourself, or assess a situation and deal with it in a rational— and successful—way. For example, "KMS" is about keeping your mouth shut, because there are times when silence is golden. "I'm not lonely when I'm alone" recognizes the fact that you have a fascinating companion with you at all times—yourself. These Magic Words and others—"Volta mind control," a way to shut out distractions, "Mirror, mirror, who the hell am I?" a quiz that makes sure we are who we want to be—are patient ways to increase your personal power.

"Magic Words You Say to Others" are best used when things get difficult with someone else—a boss, a colleague, a spouse, or just a nosy stranger. These Magic Words can avoid a prying question, end an unpleasant conversation, or defuse an argument. They also work when a friend or family member needs help coping with a divorce, an affair, a job layoff, or the infighting of office politics. Magic Words like "Let's quit while we're behind," "I want to give you another shot," "This is a pewter opportunity," and "Why are you asking?" can be show-stoppers, door-openers, and life-savers. They can prevent or re-solve difficulties in every area of our lives.

There were some Magic Words that seemed to fit a third major category. We called them "Universal Magic Words." They were words we used as philosophical cues, touchstones, and talismans—"Ego snacks" as a reminder that self-esteem should never be put on a diet; "300-second sex" to keep your love life ticking; "handle with flair" to add zest to the dull parts of daily life. They are like mantras we use to get through various sticky situations. So we started making lists of "Universal" words too.

Eventually, the three lists grew so long, and the Magic Words became so much a part of our lives, that one evening, we started talking about putting them into a book. Each of us had written books before, and we were aware of the amount of work that would have to go into the creation of this one, but the idea was compelling. We believed that if we could get it right, our Magic Words might open a door or provide a pat on the back for someone we didn't know. It was a nice thought.

Before embarking on this project we agreed to sleep on it and talk the next morning. We knew that writing a book was a little like setting out on Mao's long march: the journey would be longer and rockier than we expected. Alexandra got to the phone first. Howard was barely awake when he heard her say, "Handle with flair."

"Great," he told her, "though I feared you might say, 'I've decided not to decide,' or 'If I don't start, I don't have a prob-lem.'" But luckily she didn't. So after our long march, here are the Magic Words.

Magic Words

YOU SAY TO YOURSELF

1

CAN I SAY "I LOVE YOU" TOO MUCH?

Unless you have a compulsive disorder the answer to this Magic Word question is ABSOLUTELY NOT!

Most of us find it easy to say "Thank you." We say it without a second thought to complete strangers in supermarkets, at ball games, on the street, almost everywhere. And we say it to people we'll probably never meet again. Most of us even say "You're welcome" in response to a "Thank you." Now "I love you" is, we must admit, one word longer than "Thank you," and you don't necessarily want to say it to the supermarket checkout person. However, it shouldn't be that much more difficult to say to the people you truly care about.

We're generally able to muster the big three words at special events. It's as if "I love you" is a phrase that's supposed to be voiced only on those days that are circled on the calendar. We trot out the words at weddings, birthdays, anniversaries, graduations. But when you really care about someone, they should be everyday words. Very important everyday words.

We met Theresa years ago when she was a hostess at a restaurant we went to a lot. She was smart, funny, and warm. We quickly became friends. Now she owns her own small restaurant. Like Theresa, the place is Italian. The food is great and the prices are reasonable. That's why it quickly became a success. It's nice to have a friend with a hot restaurant, because it sure helps when you want to get a reservation.

About the time Theresa opened her restaurant, she met Malcolm. Malcolm, who's an accountant, helped Theresa set up the restaurant's books. Pretty soon the two saw that they had more in common than debits and credits, and before Theresa's Cucina celebrated its first anniversary, the two were married. They're well suited to each other and very much in love. The only problem is that Theresa used to wish Malcolm was more expressive about his feelings. He's from an old New England family where expressions of affection were always kept under wraps.

Theresa's family punctuates almost every sentence with a hug and a kiss. "I guess it's the Mediterranean influence. When I was a kid and my mother would send me out for a quart of milk, she'd say to me, 'Be careful and remember I love you.' We always said 'I love you' to each other. That's just the way we were. It's not an easy thing for Malcolm to say, but I need it. Just the way a dog has to be petted, I need an 'I love you' every day. I decided I had to wage an all-out campaign to re-condition Malcolm. I knew he'd never be like my family, but I had to move him a bit from his New England roots.

"I started to leave Post-its all around our apartment saying, 'I love you.' Some were in English, some Italian, even a couple in Chinese (I got one of my waiters to write it out for me in Mandarin). I put them everywhere: in his sock drawer, under his toothpaste, on the rearview mirror of his car. Occasionally, I would spell it out on the bathroom mirror in shaving cream. I knew he liked it, but it took a while for him to respond. Then one day as Malcolm was leaving to go to work he said it. Of course, he prefaced it by saying, 'By the way—.' It made my day. Now hardly a day goes by without an 'I love you, hon.' I don't know why it makes me feel so good, but damn it, it does."

If you want to make someone you love feel good, just say those three words. They always work.

2

IT'S THIMBLE TIME

Each of us remembers our mother taking out a basket of clothes that needed mending and spending an hour or so sewing. Like many children, we were fascinated by the little metal thing that she put on one of her fingers. The thimble. We particularly loved the word. Thimble. It's right up there among the all-time cutest words. Many years later, that word led us to these Magic Words. They've served us and our friends very well.

Jocelyn, an old friend who's an editor at a home furnishings magazine, told us the following,

"This is about Amy and me. I'd say she's one of my closest friends. We met in our sophomore year at college. We're married to guys who were in the same fraternity. Our husbands play tennis together each week. Amy and I attend the same reading group and investment club. Our houses are a block apart. And, every summer, we share a house on the Cape for two weeks. I think you'd say that makes for a pretty close friendship. I care for her immensely and I know she feels the same way.

"Amy does one thing that drives me crazy. She has a perfect figure. Or as near perfect as a woman in her forties can have. And she knows it. She also works out like she's trying for the Olympics. My body is an entirely different story. I'm not fat, but I'll admit to "full-figured." I've always been that way. My husband, Gary, likes me the way I am, and that's the most important thing. I watch what I eat and I exercise. Doesn't change a thing. I have a certain body type and Amy has another. I've discussed this with her maybe a thousand times. She says she says she understands completely. Then why does she always make little remarks about the differences in our bodies? Things like, 'Those pants look great on you, Jocelyn. I wanted to buy them, but they didn't have them in my size.' Meaning: only the larger sizes were available. Or: 'I signed up to run in the 10K race in two weeks. I wish we could do it together someday.' Meaning: Your weight will probably never permit that. This is from a woman I care for immensely. I realize that she can't help it, since I've pointed out to her what she's doing many times. Amy's not saying something terrible, but it annoys the hell out of me. So whenever she does it I say, 'It's Thimble Time.' It's as if I wrap an imaginary thimble around myself and I'm completely protected from the occasional little jabs that Jocelyn sometimes gives me. Why let a little a pinprick ruin a great relationship?"

A thimble is just the right size to protect you from small annoyances. When Robert's wife boasts, as she does too often, "I could have qualified for the Olympic ski team if I hadn't married Robert," Robert puts on the thimble and sees the statement for what it is: an attempt by his occasionally insecure wife to sound important.

A friend's niece, Carrie, told us that on her first job, she was the official coffee girl. Every morning, as she poured coffee into one man's cup, he said, "That's the way I like it. Black and bitter." "He was relentless in his repetition," says Carrie. "I began to dread the moment when he'd hold out the cup. He *always* said it. It was such a petty thing, but it made me grit my teeth." She tried Thimble Time. "I made it a game. He'd hold out his cup and *I'd* say, 'Black and bitter.' We'd each try to get it in first, and I actually began to look forward to the moment I'd pour out the coffee. The joke turned him into a friend."

The first time Howard noticed his mother's thimble, he asked her what it was for. She told him that one little jab won't hurt, but if you keep jabbing the same place, you'll have a very sore finger. Maybe Thimble Time isn't for the big things, but much of life is made up of those small ones.

3

IT'S BODY ARMOR TIME

"It wasn't my dream job, but the pay was good. In fact, it was excellent. Little did I know there was a reason the salary was so good. As someone once told me, 'They pay well in hell, too.'" This is Vince talking—a friend who lives in Orlando and works as an engineer. "I had been out of work for six months. I had a stack of unpaid bills that could have choked a giraffe. D***** Industries was a small company, sixty or so employees. The owner, Pete, who interviewed and hired me, had started the firm six years earlier. He was a smart guy. That much was obvious during the interview. But he was also a lot of other things that only came out after I started working there.

"His yelling was the least of it, and this was a man who liked to yell. Pete had a nasty streak that seemed unquenchable. He particularly liked to take people down in front of others. The first time he did it to me, at a meeting with six others at the conference table, I almost got up and hit the guy. I live by a very simple rule: I don't abuse people and I don't take abuse from people. But then I thought of my paycheck. My wife, Debbie, was still recovering from an operation and unable to work. We needed the money I made there. So I hunkered down and took it. By constantly telling myself that it was body armor time, I *almost* felt that I was wearing protection from Pete's assaults.

"I knew I couldn't take Pete's abuse indefinitely. So even though I did what everyone else in the company did—acted as his punching bag—I looked for a new job with a fervor I'd never known before. Every minute of free time was spent sending out my resume and going on interviews. It didn't take too long before it paid off. I landed a job that didn't pay quite as much, but where the boss treated me and everyone else with warmth and consideration.

"I clearly remember the day I was finally able to take off my body armor. Pete was, as usual, ripping into everyone at the weekly production meeting. He was ticking his way around the table with the relentlessness of a metronome. Finally, it was my turn. As he hurled his invective at me, I smiled at him.

" 'What are you smiling about, you incompetent?'

"I pushed a small box toward him. I had carefully wrapped it in silver paper and tied a red ribbon around it.

" 'What the hell is it?' he screamed.

" 'There are two things in there, Pete. One is a letter of resignation. I've never had as much pleasure writing anything since I sent a fan letter to Julie Christie when I was in college. The other is a set of earplugs. They really work. I've been using them since my first week here. I suggest you use them yourself. I doubt that even you like listening to the acid rain you spit out every day.'

"And with that, I stood up and left."

There are times we have to grit our teeth and take it. Like Vince, we may really need the money. Or we may be taking a required course from a terror of a teacher. In those situations, putting on body armor can help us ride out the storm. But never forget that eventually you want to remove that armor. If you meekly settle into the situation and learn to accept the abuse, you'll be wearing body armor all your life. Lugging around something that heavy every day will really wear you out.

4

VOLTA MIND CONTROL

We were at the opening of a show of paintings by the great American artist Kenneth Noland when we caught up with an old friend, another painter, whom we hadn't seen for a while—Jeannie R. We exchanged the typical New York cocktail patter, updating the events in our lives, and, of course, we told her we were writing this book. Without missing a beat, she said 'Volta Mind Control,' a phrase that conjured up a robot's gleaming titanium head exploding with flashes of lightning as an evil genius took control of it. Turns out our fantasies were about as far away as a space odyssey from what Jeannie was talking about.

Years ago when she lived in Texas, Jeannie took up tennis, practicing her strokes and her serves as often as she could. The court nearest to her was in a place called Volta Park. Whenever she had a willing partner or a spare minute to lob balls against the concrete wall near the court, Jeannie headed off to Volta. Trouble was, Volta also had several basketball courts. Fierce pickup games continued around the clock. No matter what hour Jeannie arrived at the park, people were screaming and yelling as they went up for jump shots, drove for the basket, or cheered the other players on.

Learning to play tennis, like becoming skilled at any sport, requires concentration. With hordes of basketball players and cheering groupies nearby, Jeannie was having a very tough time. Until she came up with the Magic Words. Each day as she left her house, racquet in hand, on her way to the park, she said to herself, "Volta Mind Control, Volta Mind Control." As she walked, she also visualized herself at the court with the hullabaloo of the hoopsters surrounding her, and then she willed herself into concentrating totally on what she would be doing physically. When she marched out onto the court, Volta Mind Control took over and she could single-mindedly sweat out her shots and serves.

The Magic Words were so effective that Jeannie began applying them to other situations where she needed tight focus and mental control. After she reached her studio to begin painting, she found all kinds of stray thoughts flying into her mind. Had she remembered to call the air-conditioning people? What should she buy for dinner? The hustle and bustle of daily life created mental detours and disrupted the process of painting. Volta Mind Control brought her back on track.

As Jeannie attests, Volta Mind Control is a highly effective tool for achieving self-discipline, and helps in many different situations. The process of writing, for example, is one that most of us find difficult, present authors included. Stories abound of writers who sit down to write only to jump up to sharpen dozens of pencils, wash the car, do the laundry, or balance the checkbook. We often found ourselves resorting to even more extreme avoidance tactics, but then we started using Jeannie's magic words. Volta really helped us get back to the computer clear-headed and motivated.

When extraneous thoughts or external factors like noise or commotion threaten your powers of concentration, Volta can be of immeasurable use. The key to Volta's magic is repetition, which makes the words into a kind of Pavlovian stimulus. As Jeannie found, the more you use Volta, the easier and faster your mind responds to the words and helps you stay focused. Say "Volta Mind Control," and even evil geniuses or wicked robots won't be able to keep you from winning at tennis or concentrating on the book you always wanted to write.

5

KMS

KMS is a sweet and useful little acronym that stands for Keep Mouth Shut. KMS are Julie's magic words. Julie is a young woman who was born and bred in New Orleans. She's beautiful and as delicate as a gardenia, but her charming ways often camouflage the fact that she's super-smart and seriously knowledgeable about a wide range of subjects. And she has strong opinions based on all that brainpower. She has her own point of view on everything from childbirth and cooking to affairs of state and affairs of the heart.

Take politics, for example. Julie is a staunch advocate of a woman's right to choose, a subject on which most people have definite ideas. "I used to get embroiled in these long and debilitating discussions about abortion when I went out with friends," she says, "and of course nothing was ever resolved. The only thing that changed were the friendships. Everyone went home angry.

"KMS is a great way of disengaging yourself in tricky circumstances," Julie says. "I started saying Keep Mouth Shut to myself so I wouldn't get involved in futile dialogues. I use KMS when I know that opening my mouth will have a more negative consequence than just sitting there and listening."

Julie's Magic Words work wonders when she is dealing with a combative or aggressive person. "Instead of joining their game," she says with a smile, "you just KMS and it never fails to defuse their power plays."

It's only human to have opinions and to want to make them known, just as it is natural to speak your piece when you're annoyed or frustrated. But before you speak, take a millisecond to think through the effects of your words. Decide to KMS if what you're about to say is basically unessential and serves only to escalate a situation into something unpleasant or difficult.

The world of family relationships, for example, is one where KMS has countless uses. Siblings often fall into pointless disputes or mothers and grown-up children get into unnecessary arguments when a simple application of KMS could avoid all the fuss. We think that KMS is one of the most useful Magic Words in managing all kinds of relationships.

One woman told us she was certain that one of the reasons all three of her daughters-in-law genuinely loved her was that she almost always kept mum when asked her opinion on sensitive questions. "The kids are lovely and kind and want to include me in their lives and I certainly appreciate their efforts," she says, "but I learned long ago that the best policy is to simply nod neutrally and stay out of their affairs. They want to go their own ways anyhow. If I step in with my view—even if I've been asked—it usually just complicates things. I Keep My Mouth Shut. And it keeps the peace."

6

THE BEST OFFENSE IS
MORE OFFENSE

Keeping your mouth shut isn't always the way to go. In some situations it is vitally important for you to be a pain in the ass. Let Fran, who works for an interior decorating firm, tell you why.

"Artie and I had been married for almost ten years when, during a routine annual physical, he wasn't able to complete his stress test. Not a good sign, right? The doctor found that Artie's cholesterol was too high and his blood pressure was lousy, too. He immediately put him on the right drugs to lower both of them. But Artie still had a problem that only he could solve. Artie was overweight. By a lot.

" 'Fran,' the doctor told me the next day, 'if Artie doesn't lose weight, and I mean lose it right now, he won't have to worry about whether the social security fund goes bankrupt.'

"I made an appointment for Artie to see a nutritionist, who put him on a sensible diet. Artie has been overweight most of his life. He's tried every diet from Scarsdale to Beverly Hills. And he wasn't into his new one for three days when I caught him eating a hot dog! I knew his diet absolutely didn't include eating hot dogs, so I yelled and stamped my feet and for another two days he stayed on the diet until I noticed that two pints of chocolate swirl were missing from the freezer.

" 'Artie, this is just ridiculous,' I screamed at him. 'It's suicidal. You're killing yourself. If you don't stick with this diet I'm going to . . .' At this point I stopped because I didn't know what to say that would scare him enough for him to stay the course. Should I threaten to leave him? Probably it was too early to say that. What could I say? Then it hit me. I had seen a 1940s British film the week before, and one of the characters was 'sent to Coventry': given the silent treatment. That's what I would do. I told Artie that I would stop talking to him, really stop, if I caught him cheating on his diet again. That worked for almost a week. Then I discovered that Artie had gone off the rails. Off he went to 'Coventry.' I didn't say a word to him. This time it didn't work. I soon found an empty carton of donuts in the glove compartment of his car. Silence might be golden for some, but it was absolutely tin with Artie.

"When you love someone the way I love Artie you're prepared to do anything to help them. That's why I decided to move out. I left Artie a note and told him if he wanted me back he would have to prove it. How? By getting on a scale and showing me that he had lost ten pounds. Until he could do that I would stay with my friend, Annie, who lives in the next town. It threw Artie for a loop. But you know something? It worked. Artie stayed on his diet, lost the ten pounds, and then ten more. Artie recently had another stress test, which he passed with flying colors. And I don't think I'll ever have to stay with Annie again."

When someone you love really needs your help, you may

have to toss out your normal behavior and totally "get in their face." Being a harpy, kvetch, boor, you name it, is okay if the end is important enough. So pour on the offense if the situation warrants it. The other person will not only forgive you for it, they might even love you more when it's over.

7

LET IT GO

Over the years we've asked a lot of couples what makes their marriages work. We've heard a range of answers from the slightly impractical ("I only listen to him half the time!") to the totally impractical ("I never listen to him"). We began to think that to describe marriages you needed to paraphrase Tolstoy's comment about families: "All happy marriages resemble each other; each unhappy marriage is unhappy in its own way."

Take Harriet and Bill. They've been married for almost twenty years. Both of them have strong personalities, and during the many years they've been together they've had more than their share of ups and downs. They've gone through periods of great anger where one of them "sent the other to Coventry." Silence, used as Fran used it to protect her husband's health, can be a useful tool. Used in anger it's a powerful and painful statement in a marriage. These silent periods would eventually end, and the love Harriet and Bill felt for each other would reemerge. But those times were tough on the pair. So we really wanted to know how they've been able to stay together through almost two decades. The key: some Magic Words that every one of us can put to use.

"We're both extremely stubborn. Each of us is absolutely certain that we're in the right," Harriet explained. "When we were first married we used to have terrific battles. They could be about things that were important (could we afford to buy a house) or trivial (where to place the butter knives on the dinner table). It took us more than a few years of weathering these squabbles, big and small, to hit on a solution that helped us ease the friction and defuse the anger."

"I don't know which one of us said it first, but 'Let It Go' has become the phrase that enables us to step back from the firefight and see what's more important: the love we have for each other," Bill told us. "Sometimes I fold my hands and let Harriet do it her way. Other times Harriet will do the same. Best of all, 'Let It Go' helps us reach a midpoint that works for both of us."

"Once," said Harriet, "we wrote down what arguments we'd had in the preceding three months. You know what? We couldn't remember most of them. Life's too short to fight over unimportant stuff.

"If we realize an argument is about an important issue, we mutually agree to take it off the table for a while to let our emotions settle down. Instead of 'Let It Go,' it's 'Let's Take a Break.' But just saying either set of words isn't enough. You have to act on them. You deliberately drop the issue, and you do not revisit it. This is not as easy as it sounds. If a quarrel crops up again, just repeat the Magic Words. It only takes a little while before the habit takes hold."

Letting it go benefits you both mentally and physically. As soon as you release your angry thoughts, the clouds of frustration and resentment in your head dissipate and you can go on with your life. These Magic Words can also lower your blood pressure (following a good diet and not smoking also helps). Best of all, they keep your relationship on an even keel.

8

IT'S ONLY ME

These Magic Words have been important to us since the first time we heard them. They enable us to periodically step back from the image we ordinarily project and see ourselves as we really are. We use these words regularly. They're good when times are bad. They're even better when times are good. They're the perfect splash of cold water we all need when we begin thinking we're a little better or more important than the next person.

Gerard R. Roche is the CEO of Hendrick and Struggles, the world-famous executive search firm. Roche comes from a modest background in Scranton, Pennsylvania. While serving in the army in World War I, his father contracted an illness that so debilitated him that he was unable to leave the house. But he had to earn a living to support his family. What to do? His answer was to open a small grocery store right in their living room. Whenever a customer would open the front door to enter the store—which was also the front door of the house—a bell would ring. If the family was having dinner, they would take turns getting up from the table to tend to the customer. When family members entered the house and set off the bell, they would call out, "It's only me!" so that the others would know it wasn't a customer and wouldn't have to disrupt dinner.

Gerard Roche still uses these Magic Words all the time. During both stressful and rewarding times, saying them reminds him who he is and where he came from. No matter what level of success we reach, we need to keep in touch with the person who lurks inside, the one that knows who we really are.

Saying "It's Only Me" keeps you in touch with that inner self, the one who knows what it feels like to be happy or hurt and who understands how other people feel. Remember when the frightening Wizard of Oz was revealed to be an ordinary man? He'd let the image he projected swallow up the person he really was, and he lived in dread of being found out. There's a bit of Oz in all of us, that fear that people will discover we're smaller than we seem. That's why we need these Magic Words. When you're busy e-mailing friends in order to keep in touch, take a minute to say to yourself, "It's Only Me." It's no good keeping in touch with everyone else and losing touch with ourselves.

9

SITTING ON THE FENCE IS
FINE FOR MY CAT

"Life is movement," our friend Brian always says. "When you stop moving, you stop living." He's not talking just about physical movement. What he's getting at is always giving yourself an opportunity to make a mistake. Making mistakes is what life is about. Let Brian explain.

"I used to be the kind of person who would do anything to postpone a decision. Call those years—and there were quite a few of them—my 'hammock phase.' I was addicted to just being comfortable with life, gently swinging in my hammock, away from the problems of the world. There was no decision that I couldn't put off, from making an appointment for a dental checkup, to deciding on what color to paint my bedroom, to changing my career.

"I had been working as a junior architect at a small company in Boston for three years. It was my second job since I'd left school, and the work I was doing was routine and boring. I checked all blueprints for code violations, worked on my computer to analyze material costs, that kind of stuff. Of course, I saw myself eventually designing museums in Tokyo and office towers in Los Angeles, but I certainly wasn't on that track. One day I was asked out to lunch by two friends, Dorrie and Mac, who worked with me at the company. They were basically in the same career position that I was in, and our lunches were generally taken up with lots of bitching and moaning about what we were doing.

" 'Are you really happy working here?' Dorrie asked me.

" 'About as happy as if I was in the Gulag, except the food here is better,' I answered with a laugh, as I took a big bite out of my hamburger.

" 'How'd you like to join a new firm?' asked Mac.

" 'A small, hot firm,' added Dorrie.

" 'Around here?'

" 'Yeah. They just leased some space a couple of miles down the road.'

"Then they both smiled and told me that they had decided to quit and open an office.

" 'Wow, that's great, guys.'

" 'How'd you like to join us? As a founding partner, that is,' said Mac.

"Since I was still in my hammock phase, you don't have to guess what my answer was. I told them I needed a few days to think it over and then, of course, I told them it wasn't the right time for me. Well, Mac and Dorrie set up their company, which struggled for a couple of years but gradually began to attract notice. Better yet, they were doing work that anyone would be proud of. I was happy for them, but I was also angry at myself for having lost a great opportunity. One evening I was reading on the patio behind my townhouse—in a hammock, which in retrospect seems appropriate. A neighbor's cat was sitting on the fence between our yards. He stretched, put his paws over the edge as though he were about to jump back into his yard, changed his mind, sat down again, and a few minutes later repeated the whole process. I watched him for almost five minutes before I climbed out of the hammock and pushed him back into his yard. I was making him do what I hadn't been able to do myself.

"Not long after the cat-on-the-fence incident, I got a call from Mac. Would I like to come on board? No partnership was offered this time, though there might be one down the line, but they wanted me anyway. My salary would be lower and the hours longer. But I would be doing some challenging work. How about it? It was my chance to get off the fence. That was five years ago, and I'm happy to say that I'm now a partner. By the way, I recently asked Chris, the woman I'd been living with the past four years, if she would marry me. She said yes. My neighbor's cat still sits on the fence. I don't."

A lot of us, like Brian, are a little bit lazy. But, as Brian said, you have to move. Staying in one spot, whether it's in a job or a relationship, may feel comfortable, but it will never broaden your horizons. When you think about it, sitting on a fence isn't that comfortable—unless you're a cat.

10

STRESS LEVEL NO. 5

With no warning, the board of a Fortune 500 company fired their CEO, and a new man—we'll call him Andrew Jones—was named to take his place. None of the senior people knew the incoming CEO personally or had worked with him. Months earlier the company had scheduled an offsite meeting for top executives. Even though the gathering was to take place only four days after Jones arrived on the scene, he decided to go ahead with the get-together. It would be a good way to get to know his staff.

The first item on the agenda was a roundtable discussion on stress. The executives, sitting with their morning coffee, were asked to rate their stress on a scale of one to ten, ten being the highest. Each was asked to write down the number that accurately reflected his stress level.

When everyone had complied, the moderator asked, "Whose stress level is at one?" There was general laughter and no one raised a hand.

"Two?" he asked. No hands.

"Three? Four? Four and a half?" Still no hands. At "Five," Jones began to lift his hand but brought it back down again.

"Six?" the moderator asked, scanning the room. Jones raised his hand high. He was alone.

At seven, another lone hand shot up, at eight there were a few more. Nine and ten brought out the majority of the group.

The moderator turned to the new CEO and said, "Andy, seems like your stress level is the lowest in the group. Why do you think you're at six?"

"I rated myself between five or six," he replied, "but since this is a new job with a lot to do, I'm closer to six."

"Precisely my point. You've got a major challenge on your hands, and you're rating yourself lower than anyone else here. Can you explain it to the group?"

"Well, to me, ten would be death or serious injury to my children or my wife. That would be at the top limit of stress I could take. Major health problems would be another area where I'd feel serious strain. So on a scale of one to ten, a new job is stressful, yes, but not over the top or anywhere near it."

The expert went on to make it clear that a "healthy" stress level was between four and six. "Stress can be a good thing," he explained. "It can motivate you, it can trigger solutions, stimulate creativity. Anything around three or four is too low for most people. You're not challenged at those levels. Above eight, Andy's right, that kind of stress is equated—or should be—with life's most serious problems. If you're reaching those numbers in your everyday life, it would be a good idea to check in with your regular doctor or even a therapist."

We share this story with you to illustrate that stress is caused by lots of things—mortgage payments, watching the stock market, children's scuffles—but you need to keep it all in perspective, as Andy did. Too often we think of daily stresses as overwhelming or incapacitating. Of course cumulative stress can undermine your spirits and your outlook on life. And there are times of momentary stress when you want to creep back to bed and pull the covers over your head. As a matter of fact, Alexandra did just that early one morning when:

There was no hot water.

The glass pot broke, spilling hot coffee all over the floor.

The blender exploded and plastered a banana smoothie to the ceiling.

Hurricane Augie was wreaking destruction on an expensive, newly planted lawn.

And two cockroaches crawled out of the dishwasher.

If you had asked her, after she'd emerged from her pajamas, was she stressed? She'd have given you a knowing "Stress Level No. 5" look and replied, "No more than usual."

11

I'LL SING FOR MY SUPPER,
BUT I WON'T AUDITION

Obviously, there's nothing wrong with auditions. They make up some of the best scenes in our favorite movies, and nothing is better than nailing one and getting the part. But these Magic Words have nothing to do with the world of the screen. What we're talking about here is when you're offered a job that is essentially an understudy's role. If your potential employer tells you about a position where you'll succeed the person above you in two or three years, run, don't walk, for the nearest exit. There's an excellent chance it won't happen. And, if by some stroke of good fortune it does, then there's a good chance you'll experience a couple of years of real tension and difficulty.

We're speaking from experience. A very close friend of ours, we'll call him Josh, took a job (a great one, by the way) as second in command to a fellow who had been running his company for a long time. The man who owned the company did the hiring. Everything seemed fine at the time. The perfect job at a great company. Let's hear Josh tell it.

"Before, I was running a smaller company that I had helped build. I had been there for ten years and had, with the help of a skilled and motivated group of colleagues, made the company into an innovative and highly profitable one. I was being paid well and held a fairly prominent place in our industry. Was I restless? Probably a little. I had turned down a number of offers over the years, but then came one that I couldn't walk away from. It was from the chairman of a large and respected conglomerate. He proposed that I take the executive vice president slot at one of the most important companies within the conglomerate. This job was the number two position. I would be working directly under the company's CEO, who had been running the place for twenty-five years. In a few years the chairman told me, I would become the CEO, while my predecessor gracefully retired. It sounded great, but there was a big problem. The current CEO didn't want to retire. He had been told to hire me, which is very different from choosing and grooming a successor.

"Even if he *had* hired me, it probably wouldn't have worked. Where he was inherently cautious, I was bold (he would say too bold.) Where he ran the company from a chilly pinnacle, I was more comfortable being in the midst of things. And believe me, there were other differences between the two of us that were even more glaring.

"We were uncomfortable with each other from the start. While I was trying to learn the workings of the company and getting to know the staff, he was adroitly tearing me down, both with the other key executives and, most importantly, the chairman. Another thing I hadn't taken into consideration was that this CEO had dispatched numerous potential successors over the years. He may not have owned the company, but he acted as if he did and he had no intention of stepping down. It took him two years to do it, but finally he persuaded the chairman that I had to go. He did it by lining up all the key people in the firm to say that if I succeeded him they would leave. Whether this was actually true or not doesn't matter. What matters is that it worked. I was out, and in short order another successor was hired. He was also out within a year.

"That's the last time I agreed to try out for a role," said Josh. "I'll sing for my supper, but I won't audition."

Josh's words stayed with us. When you're offered a position, and the main reason for taking it lies in the future, not the present, proceed with caution. You're not going to become a very different person during the time you wait in the wings, are you? Then why shouldn't you be given the job now? By saying the Magic Words, "I'll Sing for My Supper, but I Won't Audition," you'll never lose sight of what you're worth.

12

WHEN YOU DRAW THE LINE,
DO IT IN CEMENT

Sallie and Jim had been dating for two and a half years. Their relationship had progressed from occasional to exclusive, and they spent weekends, vacations, and holidays together. At 34, Sallie's biological clock was ticking loudly, and she wanted The Big Commitment: marriage and children. Jim thought he'd welcome a couple of kids and a warm hearth to come home to, so he finally invited Sallie to come and live with him full-time.

Sallie told Jim firmly but kindly, "Living together is not what I had in mind. I love you with all my heart. I want to get married and start a family together."

Jim replied, "You know how much I love you, but let me think about this. Can't we live together for a while and see what happens down the road?"

"I don't want to pressure you, so take some time," Sallie said, and then applied the pressure. "But I really want an answer within the month."

During the next four weeks they talked a great deal about what it would be like to start a life together. Sallie's instincts told her that Jim wanted to avoid tying the knot, but she waited patiently until the end of the month. Jim stalled again, saying he wanted to live together before marriage. My instinct was right, Sallie told herself, he'll put this off again and again, maybe forever. I don't want to be in that kind of relationship.

She decided that she had to meet the situation head-on. The next night, she told Jim, "Marry me or I'm going to find someone else who will."

Jim said incredulously, "You're forcing me into a corner."

"I'm not," she replied. "I'm just asking for love, marriage, and stability. What's wrong with that?"

"Nothing," Jim had to admit. He was silent for a while. Sallie resolutely held her tongue until he made up his mind.

"I need more time. Please, Sallie, please."

But Sallie was adamant. "Marriage is what I need, and, though I love you, I can't take any more time," she said sadly.

For a week they didn't call or see each other. Then Jim phoned, Sallie agreed to a dinner date, and they had an all-nighter of fantastic sex. Once again, he issued his live-in offer, and she said this time she was really drawing the line; the relationship was over. A couple of weeks passed, and the same dinner/lovemaking scenario took place.

Let's take a closer look at this couple. Sallie believes that Jim is commitment phobic. What Sallie can't see is that she is as much a part of the problem as he is. She issues ultimatums and then retreats. "Now or never" means nothing, because Sallie keeps extending the deadline. She's become convinced that Jim won't commit, but she plays into whatever game he needs to play. They get back together, the pattern repeats itself, and she's more miserable than ever.

No one has ever said it's easy to leave a relationship where you've loved deeply. Indeed, it is one of the most wrenching pains you can endure. But Sallie needs to say these words to herself: *When you draw the line, do it in cement.* It's only when she won't backtrack, refuses to retreat a single millimeter, that she will have the slightest chance of getting Jim to commit.

There are many other areas of male-female relationships where a line must be drawn in cement. Sue and Hal are another example. They've been married for three years, and for most of them Sue has endured Hal's explosive and irrational temper. He gets furious at the TV remote when it doesn't work and hurls it across the room. He's done the same thing with a phone that spits static at him. He swears loudly and intensely if he's fixing something around the house and the nail doesn't go into the wall at the angle he wants it to. He curses drivers on the road, cusses when the neighbor's child splashes loudly in the pool next door, and swears if the can opener doesn't go into the groove at first stab.

Hal doesn't turn his temper on Sue, but she has explained to him over and over again that she can't stand being around the irritability and intensity he brings to the smallest everyday nuisances. Things degenerated even further when Hal left his job because he and his boss couldn't get along. Money was tight, and Hal was driving Sue out of her mind with his ill humor. She began to consider a separation. She told Hal, "I've asked, begged, and pleaded with you to maintain some sort of calm around the house. I cannot live in this kind of atmosphere where you blow up or you're grouchy at the least little thing that goes wrong. You've got to chill. If you don't, I'm leaving." And then she added a version of the magic words, "I'm drawing the line on this issue. If you cross it, I have no recourse but to get a separation." She meant it. And he knew it.

Drawing the line in cement means you've taken the necessary time to understand all the consequences of your actions, and you're absolutely certain that you can live with them. Sue had drawn the line with Hal. She was prepared to take a hike if he couldn't control his temper. She was aware she would deeply miss the good things they shared, but she wouldn't miss the emotional roller coaster and poisoned atmosphere she'd lived with for so long.

Sallie finally did begin to understand that her ultimatum wasn't going to work because she withdrew it whenever Jim reached out for her. She resolved to etch the line deeply in cement. Finally, she left Jim even though she knew she would face some rough and lonely times, but she looked forward to a new, liberated life.

As it happened, Sallie did manage to hold to her ultimatum. She ended up marrying an older man who wanted to start a new family. As for Sue and Hal, he agreed to attend an anger management workshop so that he could understand, and work on, why he was so antagonistic to all things great and small. The last we heard, Sue was cautiously optimistic but still ready to pack her bags if Jim didn't learn to curb his temper. The atmosphere at home had calmed down, and they were both happier.

Ultimatums shouldn't be used often, and they shouldn't be used lightly, but "When You Do Draw the Line, Draw It in Cement."

13

PLAYING FAST AND LOOSE IS FINE ON THE FOOTBALL FIELD

We met Tommy one evening at a soup kitchen. We were volunteering there once a week, and we liked Tommy right from the start. He was lively and accessible. Always smiling, he seemed to have just received some piece of good news. Tommy was young, only a few years out of graduate school, and worked as an analyst for a large brokerage firm. He was very successful at what he did, and his career path seemed to be heading straight up. From a friend who worked with him, we heard that Tommy was the most buttoned-down guy at the firm. If he said you'd get a report on Monday at noon, you could wager your life savings that it would be on your desk at exactly that time. If you called him, it was a certainty that he'd return your call that day.

Away from the office Tommy was a different kind of guy. He liked to have a good time and played almost as hard as he worked. He hit the hottest clubs almost every night and stayed out until 3 or 4 A.M. A few hours of sleep and he'd head into the office. We're not talking about someone who fell under the influence of drugs, though he did drink—at times, perhaps too much, but no more than the rest of his friends. (Tommy's real problem was placing too many entries in the "nightlife" column of his personal ledger.) Little by little, with all this nighttime play, the buttoned-down Tommy became unbuttoned. The reports he promised were now delayed or not delivered at all. The list of his unreturned phone calls became a running joke in the office. His boss took him aside and tried to turn him around.

"We like you a lot, Tommy," he told him. "You have a chance to become a star here. But in order to do that you have to keep your extracurricular life where it belongs: on the weekend." And then the boss, a former jock, added, "Running fast and loose is fine on the football field. But not here."

He was trying to motivate Tommy to return to his old ways. To go back to being the guy everyone could count on. Not the person you could count on to screw up. We all have different folks hanging around inside ourselves, and our job is to make sure that the destructive ones don't push the better citizens to the side. Maybe it was Tommy's lack of maturity, but he couldn't harness the party guy inside. The only thing his boss's advice did was to give Tommy a line to make jokes with. We ran into him one night at a gallery opening (he'd long since abandoned the soup kitchen). When we asked what he was up to, he made a manic face and retorted, "I've been running fast and loose on the football field." He explained the line, but he saw it as a joke, the advice of a stodgy old man. The stodgy man finally fired Tommy, and he didn't last long at his next job, either. It would be nice if this tale had a happy ending. It doesn't. Tommy never did learn that playing hard and working hard all the time only succeeds in the movies. The last we heard, Tommy was still bouncing from job to job. Playing Fast and Loose.

14

WHY AM I SMILING WHEN
I FEEL ANGRY AS HELL?

"I can't get over my anger until I recognize three things," says Vivian, a woman from Milwaukee that we met recently. "First off, I don't kid myself that I'm not really angry. It's a strong emotion, and I won't call it something else. Words like "irritation," "annoyance," or "displeasure" don't scratch the surface of anger. Secondly, I never procrastinate when I'm dealing with it. Anger is like strong coffee; unless you deal with it quickly, it'll keep you up at night. And thirdly, I recognize exactly why the anger has me in its grip. A lot of times, it's anger at myself, but it's easier to handle if I aim it at another person. Dealing with myself is never a picnic, but sometimes that's where the problem is.

"Now there are a number of things I try to avoid when I'm angry. I don't luxuriate in it. What do I mean by that? Well, anger can be very seductive. It can become the center of your life. It can keep you from dealing with other things that are more important, tough things you don't want to confront. In these situations, anger is a comfort zone. Another thing I avoid is putting up a facade as to how I feel. I take a minute to think it over, and if I still want to kick someone in the butt (figuratively, I mean), then, damn it, I'm going to do it. And if it's my own butt that needs a firm boot, then that's where the kick will go. The only facade I like are on buildings. Don't kid others about how you feel, but, more importantly, don't kid yourself."

Ask yourself this question: am I a "facade" person? Someone who disguises the level of volcanic rumbling inside and insists on showing the outside world a surface as placid as a pond? Now this isn't a bad approach if a large, dangerous animal is circling you. Not showing your true feeling—utter fear—makes sense in that situation. But when someone has done something that is thoughtless, inconsiderate, or harmful to you, let them know how you feel. Though you might like to, we don't advocate putting on your judo belt. You don't have curse or yell, just tell them what you think. There's a way to express your feelings without getting violent or overly emotional. If you find yourself repressing your feelings, ask yourself, "Why Am I Smiling When I Feel Angry as Hell?" You can never be an honest person until you start being honest with yourself.

15

ANYONE CAN SCREW ME ONCE
(I SAID ONCE!)

We're sorry for the vulgarity, but the word absolutely conveys the point of these Magic Words. No matter how perceptive you are in judging people, you'll never bat a thousand. The woods are full of charming and friendly liars. We're not talking about professional con men and flimflam artists. These Magic Words won't help if you get into their clutches. These words are directed at the liars, the gross exaggerators, and the fabricators that pass in and out of our lives.

Terry owns a travel agency in Detroit. She's very hard-working and personable, and in the ten years since she's started the business, it's grown into a successful and highly profitable enterprise. The agency has done so well that she rewarded herself by buying a small condominium on the beach in Florida. Whenever she gets a chance, she flies down there for a long weekend to break the monotony of the Detroit winter. Since the place sits empty most of the time, Terry, who's an extremely generous person, frequently lets her friends use it.

Recently, she let a new friend named Joanie stay at the apartment. Terry has this down to a science. She has a written set of instructions listing things guests need to know about (air-conditioning, how to contact the building manager, etc.) and an extra set of keys she sends to whoever is going to use the place. Typically for Terry, there are extra pages with the names of her favorite restaurants, the cab company she recommends for the trip to the airport, and the name of a doctor in case of an emergency. She also arranges for the housekeeper she employs to have fresh flowers and a bottle of wine in the fridge awaiting her guests.

Terry had met Joanie at her gym, and they discovered that they had a lot of interests in common. This led to a few dinners, and when Terry told Joanie of the condo, Joanie responded by saying, "God, I wish I had a place like that." Terry instantly offered Joanie the chance to stay there.

The next day Joanie called and gave her a date, only a week off, when she'd like to use the condo. Terry said that was fine and sent over the instructions and the keys. When Joanie got back to Detroit, she called to thank Terry for the marvelous time she'd had. She asked when Terry was going to use it next. In a month, she answered. Anyone else using it? Joanie asked. Not until after I get back, answered Terry.

A month later, when Terry finally flew down to Florida, she ran into Ted, a neighbor who lived on the floor above. After they exchanged pleasantries, Ted casually mentioned that Terry's friend must be thinking of buying a place down there. "What do you mean?" she asked. He said that since she'd come down twice in the past month, he'd assumed she must be looking for a place of her own. Twice? Why yes, he answered, I talked to her for a few minutes both times. Ted then went on to describe Joanie.

When Terry returned to Detroit, she called Joanie and made a date for dinner the next night. At the end of the dinner, Terry handed her a small gift-wrapped box.

"What's this for?"

"Open it and you'll find out," said Terry, with a smile.

Joanie quickly ripped off the paper and opened the box. Inside was a set of keys.

"What's this?" she asked.

"It's another set of keys to my condo. You can add them to your collection, Joanie. I don't need them since I've changed the locks."

"I don't understand," said Joanie.

"Unfortunately, you understand all too well," said Terry, getting up from the table. "I've taken care of the check. Why don't you have an after-dinner drink on me."

And with that Terry walked out of the restaurant.

Each time we're taken in by someone, whether it's a financial or emotional betrayal or, as in Terry's case, a betrayal of trust, we have to act quickly and decisively. We first have to admit that we've been had. The only people who haven't been treated this way at one time or another have never set foot outside their houses. So admit it. The person screwed you. But just once. They don't realize that you've used the Magic Words on them. Presto! Just like that, they'll never be able to do it to you again. They might not realize it, but they've lost a lot more than you have.

16

I'LL TAKE THE NEXT FLIGHT OUT

Alexandra had just broken up a long-term relationship, her bank account was anemic, her writing career was at a complete standstill, and she had no idea what the coming months—or years—held for her.

One night she went out with a girlfriend to see *A Room with a View*. They both loved every frame of it. Afterward they lingered late over dinner to talk about the film and the gorgeous Tuscan countryside where it took place. When Alexandra finally reached home, she climbed into bed and started to read a magazine. Just as she was about to turn off the light and call it a night, she spied an ad on the back pages:

Italy, Central Florence, Santa Croce, beautiful one-bedroom flat in palazzo with modern kitchen and bath. Will let by the month, leave message at 00-39-33-356-574.

Visions of cathedrals, paintings by old masters, fresh pasta, and homemade gelati led to a severe case of insomnia. At 4 A.M.—ten in the morning Florence time—she turned on the light and dialed the number. Within five minutes she had rented the apartment for the month of August. The next morning she mailed a sizable check for the month's rent and security and booked her flight.

Time slipped by quickly, and Alexandra soon found herself on a 747 headed for Italy. Then she panicked. *What the hell am I doing? Do I have any idea why I'm doing this?*

Two glasses of wine did nothing to allay her anxieties, which mounted when she thought about all the money she had spent on a place she knew absolutely nothing about.

"What have I done?" she thought. "Only the ad said the apartment was beautiful. It could be like the Black Hole of Calcutta. The photos looked good, but who can really tell from photos? My surroundings mean so much to me, and if it's not really lovely and comfortable, I'm going to be miserable. And I've spent way too much money on it. I need to earn a living. I should be staying in New York and trying to come up with a book idea. Whatever possessed me to be so impetuous?"

Then she decided to activate her "good cop" subconscious to counter the voice of her inner "bad cop." *You wanted adventure, didn't you? You wanted to change your life, you wanted to get over the breakup, you wanted to experience a new place.*

But the bad cop retorted, "Who are you kidding? This could be a disaster."

And then the Magic Words for this situation came to her: *If I don't like it, I'll just take the next flight out.*

What Alexandra had forgotten, like most of us who make a speedy decision, is that we always have options. She really wasn't locked into staying in the apartment, or even in Florence, for that matter. She could always take the next flight back. Sure, she'd be out of some cash, but it would be better than suffering in a bad situation for a whole month.

But of course things worked out. Wonderfully. The apartment's terrace, surrounded by climbing roses, was like something out of a dream and the sixteenth-century frescoes on the ceilings made her feel as if she were living in a luxurious museum. She came up with a book idea, and (this was not in the ad) she met a great guy.

There's more to the story. The manuscript she had been working on was called *How to Make Love to a Man*. When she came back to New York, she finished it and sold it. When the publication date neared, she was informed that in order to promote the book, she was expected to go on a nationwide publicity tour and appear on talk shows.

Writing about sex had been tough, but *talking* about it on TV in front of millions of men and women was a terrifying thought. She steeled herself by working with a coach, who helped her deal with on-camera jitters.

As luck would have it, her first interview was on a late-night show with a host who was notorious for his attack methods. Standing in the greenroom, waiting to be introduced, Alexandra tried to fight off the panic she felt. She thought back to all that her coach had taught her, but nothing worked to relieve the anxiety. Until she remembered her flight to Italy.

"I'll just take the next flight out," she said to herself. "If I walk onto that stage and it's too terrible I'll just get out of my chair and walk straight out the door and back into my regular life."

The second she realized that she had an alternative plan—an escape route from the host's verbal pummeling—she began to relax.

She walked onto the set, smiled hello to the millions of people who were watching, and faced her first question. All her fears had been unfounded. The host, like most men, was very interested in this provocative new book, and the interview went by in a flash.

Alexandra's Magic Words work in any situation, from mildly sticky to crucial. If you're having a truly miserable time at a cocktail party or on a blind date, if you've taken on a job or a project that is holy hell, even if you're at the altar and you can't go through with it, just take the next flight out and head back home. Unless you're six feet under or totally lost in outer space, you've got a lot of options. Use them.

17

I DON'T THINK I WANT YOU
IN MY LIFEBOAT

We use these Magic Words periodically as an exercise to figure out where our friends stand in our buddy batting order. Let's take Ginny first. Here's the scene: we're in a car driving to a restaurant outside the city. None of us have been there before. It's dark and the road is lightly traveled. The directions we have seem clear enough, but we still haven't found the place.

GINNY: I think we should have turned off on the road we just passed.

DRIVER: The directions say that we have to come to a crossroads, and we're not there yet.

GINNY: We've been driving for quite a while.

DRIVER: Just two and a half miles. The directions say it's three and a quarter to the crossroads.

GINNY: We're lost.

DRIVER: How can you say that? So far the directions are right on the money.

GINNY: I just know we're lost. We should pull over and go back. We'll never get there.

DRIVER: Here's the crossroads. We just turn to the left and

in a quarter mile we'll be there. Yes. I see the light from the sign now. There's the place right there.

It's pretty easy to see why we wouldn't want Ginny in our lifeboat. She's always ready to throw in the towel. Imagine being out there in a small boat in the middle of the ocean with Ginny chanting her mantra of: "They'll never find us," "We don't have a chance," and "We're going to die out here." Ginny is a good person, but this failing of hers is a serious one. She's not the friend you would want to seek out when you're in a high-pressure situation. So there's no chance we'd want her in our lifeboat.

Then there's Mario. He's rock steady when it comes to difficult times. But he has another kind of shortcoming. Let's set the scene. We're having a picnic at the beach. Everybody has an assignment. Someone is bringing the sandwiches. Someone else the beverages. Mario's responsibility is the dessert. He's supposed to bring a bunch of tarts from a new Belgian bakery that's opened near his apartment. Lunch is spread out. The sandwiches are great—little ones made of white bread with the crusts cut off. You know the kind. The drinks are first-rate. Everything from Coke to a chilled bottle of Sancerre. Now for the dessert. Mario unwraps the tarts. Surprise! No tarts.

MARIO: I didn't have time to stop at the bakery.
ONE OF US: But isn't it next door to where you live?
MARIO: Something came up.
ONE OF US: What?
MARIO: Something. (He now unwraps the box of desserts he's brought: cupcakes purchased in a convenience store. They look kind of stale. But wait a second. Two

49

of the wrappers are empty, they have already been consumed by Mario!)

Mario is someone else you wouldn't want in your lifeboat. He's both selfish and irresponsible.

When we're planning parties or joint holidays, or when business pressures eat up our time and we have to decide who we will always want to see, we use the Magic Words as a shortcut. It's easy to make an instant decision when we visualize ourselves and our friends in a lifeboat on a tossing sea. If your experience is like ours, you'll find that you still want a good percentage of your friends to be in your lifeboat. In fact, if you're lucky and have the right friends, you might even have to lower a second boat.

18

I ONLY NEED ONE

The dating situation can become pretty desperate, especially if you're a woman in your thirties and your biological clock feels like the ball that descends on Times Square on New Year's Eve. Both of us have close female friends who are single. One of them, Jackie, discovered these Magic Words that she declares cut out a lot of the stress of searching for the perfect mate in New York City.

"Even if you're a model with a Ph.D., it's not easy to find a guy in this town," claims Jackie. (We've heard similar versions of this lament from women in San Francisco, Dallas, Boston, Washington, D.C., Kansas City, and Seattle.)

"I've done everything I can think of to find guys who might be 'suitable,'" she says. "Friends told me to go to museums and strike up a conversation with a man and discuss a painting. Or they said I should take up skiing or golf or volleyball or pool—any activity that men might do by themselves or with their buddies. I've practically gone broke with memberships and tons of gear, with zero results. I've put ads in magazines and on the net, and I had a flurry of activity but nothing lasting came of it. I could go on and on about what

I've done to meet men. At one point I even tried a singles bar. *Never again!"*

Jackie is 33 and a top editor at a New York publishing house. She's not beautiful, but she definitely makes the most of what she has. Her hair is long and shiny, she watches her diet, works out regularly, and dresses with taste. She's attractive, smart, and stylish. And because she's our friend, we also know that she's warm and decent and has a great sense of humor. Plus she makes a mean pasta Amatriciana and whips up a sinful chocolate mousse as fast as you can say "marriage material."

So, what's keeping Jackie from finding a man? Absolutely nothing, except her point of view.

We'll get back to her in a minute, but now consider Karen, who happens to be a buddy of Jackie's. They work in the same office and she too is in the market for a man, but her first priority is finding a place to live. The lease on her present apartment is running out, and the landlord is jacking up the rent so high that she can't afford to renew. She wants to stay in the thick of things so she'll be more likely to meet a mate, but she's looked at dozens of apartments and each one has something wrong with it. Mostly, the places are dark and small, and the rents are outrageous. She reluctantly searched the outer boroughs—Brooklyn, Queens, Staten Island—and found a few possibilities, but when she was a young girl in Minneapolis she always dreamt of living in Manhattan and that's what she's determined to do.

"This city is apartment hell," she says. "I know all the tricks—get the Sunday real estate section of the *New York Times* on Friday, go up and down each street asking the supers whether something is coming up—I've tried every angle I can think of. And still no apartments."

One evening after work, the two women got together for

a drink. After they'd exhausted all the office gossip, they turned to Karen's apartment problem. "You really only need one," Jackie said, trying to comfort her friend. "It's not as if you have to find *three or four* apartments that are right for you. If you had to get more than one you'd be right to go crazy. But *you only need one*. Maybe if you think of it that way it won't seem so overwhelming."

They continued to chat and, of course, began discussing men.

"Men are impossible! I'm just about to give up," Jackie said. Karen immediately retorted, "Men. You don't need 'men,' plural. We're making it too complicated. We don't want a whole bunch of guys. Each of us can only use one."

Therein lie some Magic Words that can help change your point of view and lighten your load. You may need several friends and doctors and baby-sitters, but if you're searching for a big-ticket item like a mate or an apartment or a house or a job, how many are really necessary? It's a whole lot easier to find one good man than it is to find three. When a second round of white wine arrived at the table, Karen lifted her glass and toasted, "You only need one, girlfriend."

By the way, we thought you might like to know that every friend of ours who swore she'd "never find a man" ended up with a good guy. All it took was a simplified focus and a little more time.

19

MOPE OR COPE? IT'S REALLY AN EASY CALL

This seems like a no-brainer, but it's a lot more difficult than it looks. Why? Because moping around is both easy and, in a strange way, comfortable. It's like wearing that old sweater with holes at the elbows that looks like hell but feels like a second skin. Coping, on the other hand, is difficult. Imagine getting out of bed on a very cold day to discover that the furnace has given out. You can see your breath hang in the air. You can't find your slippers, and the floor is colder than an ice rink. Later, when you've finally gotten the heat situation worked out and you're sitting in the kitchen having a hot cup of strong coffee, you feel very good. Maybe you haven't conquered Everest, but you've done something very satisfying. You've coped, and you've come out on top.

We polled our friends, family, and colleagues for their thoughts on moping and their anti-mope techniques. Here's a sampling (though you have to realize we don't endorse all of them):

Our friend Brendan says, "The most important thing is to realize that you are actually moping around. That's not as easy as it sounds. A true mope has a cause, and it's not having eaten or drunk too much the night before. One's called indigestion and the other a hangover. A mope is altogether different, and you have to figure out what's causing it before you can fix it.

"Once I understand that I'm in the grip of a mope, I immediately do something fast and easy that makes me feel good. For instance, I watch an episode of *The Simpsons*. That generally works. A long, hot shower isn't bad, either. But then you have to deal with the roots of your mope. A long walk is the way I go about grappling with it. When I've found out why I'm moping around, I set a time limit on how long I'm going to allow myself to feel that way. If I feel real lazy, I'll give it a day. Never more than that. After all, I have other things to do than just mope around the house."

Alice offers this: "You have to recognize that this is something that happens to all of us. Even my cat, Jasper, mopes sometimes. I'm not talking about being depressed—that's something totally different. When you're depressed there's a good chance you need professional help. Actually, I sometimes enjoy moping around. To me, it's a state where you feel sorry for yourself, but not too sorry. A manicure will generally brighten the picture for me, or I'll go to a good movie. Scrambled eggs and toasted English muffins almost always work. Finding out why I'm moping can sometimes be difficult. I once traced it back to something a friend said to me at dinner. It was an observation about my weight—just the kind I don't need. I guess we're all sensitive to something."

Stella adds this: "When I realize that I'm moping, I ring a major alarm bell. I just don't have time for it. Moping is like listening to music through bad speakers. Who needs it? I don't even like the word. Coping is what life's about. Coping with some things is difficult, but I've learned in the past that putting it off only increases the time you're in a sorry state. In the alphabet, 'cope' is closer to 'hope,' so now that's where I always head."

That's the big difference: ultimately, coping will make you feel good about yourself. Moping? When you figure out what you get out of moping, we have a case of champagne, chilled, waiting for you.

20

THERE ARE BETTER THINGS
TO TAKE A CHANCE ON
THAN LOTTERY TICKETS

Hey, we have nothing against lottery tickets. When the jack-pots get really big, we often buy a few tickets ourselves. We always join the office pool for the Super Bowl, and, we must admit, neither of us can walk through a casino without shaking hands with the one-armed bandit or having a brief turn at the blackjack table. These are the small chances that most of us take. The problem is that some people confuse risk with chance and, intimidated by the first, are afraid to try the latter.

Teddy is an executive with an insurance company. We met him some years ago through mutual friends, and we liked him immediately. He's got a good sense of humor, and he's a kind and thoughtful person. Teddy's problem is that he's chance phobic. He's always asking us whether he should go on a trip to Vietnam, or take that new job that's been offered to him. Or whether he should move in with Anne, whom he's been dating for over a year. But Teddy never goes beyond asking for people's opinions. After he's consulted with everyone he can think of, he stops. He doesn't go on that trip. He doesn't take the job. He doesn't move in with Anne.

Our friend Christine is Teddy's exact opposite. Christine, who is an architect, is a risk addict. She's never met a risk she didn't like. Relocate for a new job after only one meeting with the company head? She's on her way. You've heard of a highly speculative stock that might be a big winner? Call Christine. She'll round up whatever money she has and pour it into the stock. You know of a diet that promises a lot but seems medically dangerous? Christine would love to be thin, so don't hesitate to ring her up. Christine has had some luck with the risks she's taken over the years, but that luck has been more than offset by the losses caused by her recklessness.

While Teddy is scared to take a chance, Christine courts risk. And there can be a difference between a chance and a risk. Saying the Magic Words "There Are Better Things to Take a Chance on Than Lottery Tickets" will remind you to make a distinction between things that probably will work and things that are a one-in-a-million long shot. Think of risk as the bigger, tougher brother of chance, something which usually involves higher stakes. Risk is where you double your money or lose it all. Risk is an untested medicine that might save your life—or end it. In life, risk is something that you should treat with caution. But chance, that's the thing that can give life zing, and when it's an intelligent, well-thought-out move, it can be the fuel that propels you in a new and better direction.

21

HOLD ON! I THINK I'M READY TO LIGHTEN UP: #1—THE FOLKS

They were there first and spent more time with us than anyone else, until the time we no longer had a curfew. Mostly, we remember that they said "No" an awful lot. We generally don't remember the sacrifices they made for us, but we sure remember the punishments they meted out, whether they were deserved or not. All of us have unresolved issues with our parents, and the lucky ones work them out while their folks are hale and hearty.

Let's go back to where this all started: you came into the world. No matter what your problem with the folks is, don't ever forget this: they didn't decide to conceive you in order to perform hideous experiments on you, like some evil Doctor Mengele. In most cases it started with love. Maybe they couldn't quite pull it off, but they honestly wanted to love and cherish you. They probably still do. Maybe things went off the tracks somewhere. But, hey, the engine is still there! Sure it's a bit battered, but it's still puffing out some smoke. And the tracks! They're torn up, but if we can repair them and fix the engine maybe we can get this thing running again. The ride won't be the smoothest, but it's still one we all should take.

Karen, a friend from college, is a successful real-estate broker in New Jersey. She's married with her first child on the way. She has two siblings, a brother and a sister. The unusual thing is that her sister and brother are twelve and fourteen years younger. They were the "change of life" children, the "happy accidents," as her parents always called them. So, in a sense, Karen was an only child.

"I love my brother and sister, and in many ways I was sort of their surrogate parent. My mother needed help with them, and I didn't mind at all. I baby-sat, fed them, changed them. What bothered me then, and still bothers me now, is that they were always treated totally differently from the way I was. They could do almost anything they wanted without the slightest rebuke. They got away with murder. I, on the other hand, always had curfews that were totally ridiculous, allowances that had to have been devised in the Middle Ages, and praise that came about as regularly as snow in Florida. Now don't get me wrong, I love my parents. They are caring and compassionate. But we hardly have a single visit that doesn't include some form of criticism. I'm spending too much on clothes, I'm becoming too thin. . . . you get the idea.

"One day when we were driving to their house to celebrate Thanksgiving, Jamie—that's my husband—said to me, 'Let's have an unusual visit this time.'

" 'What do you mean?'

" 'I know it won't be easy, but could you be a different Karen this time?'

" 'What do you mean?'

" 'Instead of being annoyed and angry when they criticize you—which you can bet they will—why don't you just lighten up and enjoy it a bit?'

" 'Enjoy being criticized?'

" 'Try to understand this. Your folks just have a peculiar

way of saying they love you. They do it with criticism. You do know they love you, right? You've told me that many times. And I know it's true. I know they express their love differently to your brother and sister, but, hey, that's life. Just lighten up and enjoy them. They're really good people.'

"It wasn't easy, but I followed Jamie's advice. When my mom said to me that she thought the earrings I was wearing didn't look right with my dress, I got up and went to the mirror in the living room. I came back and told her she was right (she actually was!). She looked at me as if she were in shock and didn't criticize me again during the entire dinner. Since that time, I've stopped being annoyed with my folks about all those little things, and, unbelievably, the criticism from their end is way down."

These Magic Words even work for those of us who have great relations with our folks. Because no matter how much love and affection there is on both sides, there will always be times when you're unable to communicate with them. Say these words to yourself at those times and loosen up toward the people who opened the door for you. It's something you'll all be grateful for.

22

HOLD ON! I THINK I'M READY TO LIGHTEN UP: #2—THE EX-SPOUSE

A lot of marriages break up leaving memories we'd like to forget but can't. No one needs that much heavy baggage to lug through life.

Dick, a college friend who lives in Toledo, found a way to let go. Recently he came across an album of photographs from his first marriage. He hadn't looked at them for ten years.

"At first, I was almost afraid to open it. Peggy and I were married for five years, half of them awful. I didn't want to revisit that period. Though I still had some good feelings about Peggy, our marriage had been a war zone. If you're lucky, you survive that kind of experience and learn something from it. On the other hand, you're not too interested in going back there for a holiday.

"As I slowly turned the pages, I was overcome by a whirl of conflicting emotions: happiness, anguish, warmth, elation, depression. You name it, they were all there. Luckily, there were more pictures from the beginning, the 'happy' period, than there were from the later years. Maybe, unconsciously, we didn't want to document the tough times. I started to remove every image from the album that reminded me of the good times Peggy and I had had. Picnics, days at the beach, feeding the pigeons in the Piazza San Marco. Good, sunny images. I tossed the rest of the photos, those with strong negative associations, out. Right into the old circular file. Once that wastebasket was full, I went to the local photo shop and had the other pictures copied. I sent them on to Peggy with a short note that said, 'I found these and they made me remember that some of our times together were pretty good. Hope you're well and flourishing, and that these might provide a happier trip down memory lane.'

"Peggy's remarried now, as am I, and though we're not in touch much, I think she's happy. I got a letter back from her a week later saying that the photos had made her feel good. I think that doing that, editing the photos and sending them on, finally put that experience into perspective for me."

All marriages begin with something good. It's a shame to forget that, and if there are kids, it's imperative for you to let them know that at one time their parents were in love. So when you begin to remember the bad things, Lighten Up. Remember that some things were good.

23

HOLD ON! I THINK I'M READY TO LIGHTEN UP: #3—THE SIBLING(S)

He (or she) broke your toys. He lied to your mother, blaming you for things he did, and you were the one who got punished. He was favored a lot of the time (you were, too, but you've forgotten that by now). He always got away with murder (you only got away with manslaughter).

You're both adults now, sort of. But his sibling rap sheet is still current in your mind. He probably doesn't steal your toys anymore, nor does he tell lies about you to your mother. So why don't you take a look at him now without the grade-school silliness clouding your view? He's probably got more than a few virtues, which you can sometimes recognize at family gatherings. But you generally don't dwell on them. He still looks like the nemesis you remember when you were both kids, except he now has a gut (which secretly pleases you) and is losing his hair (which pleases you even more because you know that it bothers the hell out of him). Isn't it time to occasionally give him a genuine hug? To thank him for something he did a long time ago that was really important to you? There's too much you both share to go through the rest of your life thinking of him just as a former roommate. You love your parents equally. You're sure of that. There'll come a time when something important comes up and you'll call him. And in your heart of hearts, you know that he'll be there for you, too.

Gail, a friend from college, was brought up in a suburb of Chicago. Now in her late thirties, she has a younger brother named Jack. They had many fights—countless, says Gail—while they were growing up.

"Jack was a shit as a kid. No, let me amend that. He was a perfect shit. From the time he was a toddler, he seemed to catalog everything that might bother me and then proceed to do it. Unless I remembered to hide my science project, he'd break it. When I started to date, Jack would barge in on me and my boyfriends every minute on the minute until we were forced to leave the house. It was impossible to bring boys home unless Jack was on a class trip or playing in a Little League game. We actually started to have a semblance of a relationship when he hit his teens, but then I was off to college. Of course, he's not a little terror now, but that's what I remember about him. It's been a real barrier to our getting close—something neither one of us could bridge. Then, two years ago, our Mom got sick and died within three months. I was devastated. So was Jack. We both spent a lot of time with our dad, helping him get through it. It was the first time since we were kids that Jack and I had seen a lot of each other. I suddenly saw that Jack was a great guy. Jack the brat only existed in the cobwebs of my memory, and I realized that I was lucky to have a brother like him. The distance between us was created by my inability to let go of childhood quarrels. I just had to step back, lighten up, and look at him as he is now. I lost my mother, but I gained a brother."

Sometimes a relationship—like the one between Gail and

her brother—needs a strong jolt to help two people see each other for what they are now, not what they once were. These Magic Words will help you lighten up your attitude toward someone with whom you shared so many important years of your life.

24

HOLD ON! I THINK I'M READY TO TIGHTEN UP: #1—THE BOSS

We've already talked about the need to lighten up, so here's the first of three Magic Words that are about times when things are just the opposite: when it's necessary, even imperative, to tighten up. We'll start with someone most of us have to deal with at one time or another—the boss. The following was told to us by our friend, Harvey.

"I'd been working at my new job for about a year. The company was midsized, and I was slotted third in the pecking order, a jump for me. The company was owned and run by the guy who started it, Ray. Ray was a hard-charging guy who worked insane hours but didn't expect the rest of us to do the same. The pay was good, and I enjoyed working closely with him. He certainly wasn't a yeller, and most of the time he had a pretty good sense of humor. As far as my job went, I was as satisfied as I had ever been. But I did have one problem with Ray that bothered me a lot.

"It started as I was leaving the office one Friday, a month or two after I began working there. It was just past six, and I stopped in to see Ray about a call I had gotten from a client. Ray, of course, was at his desk. We talked for a few minutes about the client, and as I stood up to leave, Ray asked me a question.

" 'Harv, could you do me a favor?'

" 'Sure, Ray. What do you want?'

" 'I'll be here at least another couple of hours, and I need to pick up a suit I just bought that's been altered. I want to wear it at a wedding I'm going to over the weekend. The shop will be closed when I get out of here. Think you could pick it up for me?'

" 'No problem, Ray.'

"And it wasn't a problem. The store was only ten minutes out of my way, and Ray lived a few blocks from me. What *was* a problem was that this was the beginning of a long string of favors and chores that Ray asked me to do for him. Things like checking on his house when he was away on one of his rare vacations, dropping off his car at the garage for an oil change, picking up theater tickets for him because he heard I was going to be downtown. None of these 'favors' was demeaning or over the line, but there were a lot of them and they were beginning to annoy me. I knew that if I didn't talk to Ray soon, the annoyance would ratchet up to something that could sour our working relationship. I stayed late one day so I could catch Ray without the phone ringing.

" 'Do you have a minute, Ray?' " I asked, as I walked into his office. As fate would have it—and this is something you would never accept in a novel or movie—Ray actually started asking me to do him a favor. He slid a small envelope across his desk. He explained that it contained his watch, which needed a new battery. Since he had to be in the office very early the next day for a meeting, could I drop it off? I looked at the envelope for what felt like a long time without speaking.

" 'I'd be happy to do it this time, Ray,' " I said, putting the envelope in my pocket. I then went on to tell him how much I liked him and the entire atmosphere at the company. And then I got to my problem. Though I was happy to help him out, I was beginning to feel that his endless 'string of favors' was getting out of hand. I told Ray that being his senior V.P. and colleague was enough without tacking on the job of executive assistant. I was prepared to say either errand boy or manservant but switched at the last moment. Ray said he understood and reached across the desk to shake my hand. Had I overstepped the line? I kept asking myself as I drove home. The following day went smoothly. Ray and I had a series of meetings, and everything felt normal to me. Even though I thought I had said the right thing to him, I still had some fear that I had damaged our relationship and, perhaps, jeopardized my job. My fears vanished that evening when I left the office. I almost walked past my car in the parking lot. It absolutely gleamed. There was a handwritten note stuck under the windshield wiper. It was from Ray.

" 'Thought your car needed a little washing. I got the keys from your wife. It's one small payback for all you've done for me. What you said last night registered with me. It's a bad habit I have. You're not the first to point it out. I will work on it. You're important to the company, and I sure don't want you to leave, Ray.' "

Your boss is an important and powerful figure in your life—and always will be. That makes it hard to draw the line when an employer oversteps his bounds. But relationships work best when they're conducted on the right basis. Don't be afraid to use these Magic Words to Tighten Up a relationship with your boss when it moves off the proper track. It will turn out to be good for both of you.

25

HOLD ON! I THINK I'M READY TO TIGHTEN UP: #2—THE FRIENDS

You might think it's easier to deal with your friends than with your boss, but that's not always the case. They can ask too much, too, and because we're afraid of seeming ungenerous, we often accede.

We've known Kent since he moved to New York. We don't see him as much as we'd like since he and his wife, Annie, moved to the suburbs, but when he told us this story of a friendship almost gone aground, we knew that these Magic Words would work for him.

"Yes, we miss the city, but living here in the burbs has its pluses," Kent told us. "One of them is that small-town life makes for different, and sometimes deeper, friendships. Annie and I met Rita and Gene in a Lamaze class right after we moved here. Our children were born within a week of each other, and from that moment on Rita and Gene became our best friends.

"Rita became Annie's buddy, and Gene is my golfing partner and the guy I watch all important football games with. We commute together, and the four of us have even gone to Europe twice. It's a given that no matter how much you like a person, they will always have some trait that drives you a little nuts. Gene, though I really love the guy, has one in spades. Gene regards everything that's mine as his. In the beginning it didn't bother me. Then it was mostly small things—he'd borrow a tie or a hedge clipper. He'd return the tie when it had gone out of style, and the hedge clipper when it broke. If he saw a book that interested him, it was under his arm and on his night table before I could say, 'Why don't you take a look at that, Gene.' Then it sort of naturally progressed to bigger things, like money and my car.

" 'I'm a little short this week, Kent,' he'd say. 'Could you spare a hundred?'

" 'You still owe me the two hundred you borrowed last month, Gene,' I'd say with a slight edge in my voice.

" 'Jesus, Buddy, when did you suddenly become an accountant? You know I'm good for it.'

"Gene's car also seemed to wind up in the garage with maddening regularity.

" 'I need new brake linings, Kent. Could I borrow your car this afternoon?'

" 'What about your wife's?'

" 'She's using it. I only need it for an hour or so.'

" 'How about me dropping you off where you have to go? I have an appointment for a haircut.'

" 'Can you change it? I'll have it back to you in no time.'

"I had reached the point where my anger at Gene was starting to crowd out my affection for him. I knew I had to tighten up this aspect of our relationship soon. Real soon. I found the opportunity one day when Annie told me that Gene had called once again about borrowing my car. He'd have it back in an hour, he told her. When she told him she would not be in the house when he got there, Gene told Annie that was no problem. He knew where I kept the extra set of keys!

I got home before Gene arrived. I took my extra set of keys from a bowl in the kitchen where I kept them and replaced them with a set from my last car. I then got into Annie's car and rode around with her while she did her errands. When I got back, I found a frustrated Gene sitting behind the wheel of my car futilely trying to get the wrong keys into the ignition. I invited him inside for a beer, and we had a long, serious discussion. I told him our friendship was important to me and, I believed, to him, too. Therefore, I could no longer put up with Gene's loose concept of 'borrowing.' At first, he was insulted. His voice was raised, but then so was mine. Two beers later I think we both understood each other better. I could never stop Gene from being Gene, but in the future if one of his requests bothered me, I said that not only would I tell him, but he should be prepared for me to say no. The improvement came slowly, but it came. And, most important of all, we're still friends."

We all need to draw lines around ourselves. They're an intangible expression of Robert Frost's "Good fences make good neighbors." Like real fences, our personal barriers sometimes sag and need to be tightened up. Yes, it's scary to "tighten up" on a friendship; what if you lose the friend? But if it can't survive the Magic Words "Tighten Up," it's not the friendship you thought it was.

26

HOLD ON! I THINK I'M READY TO TIGHTEN UP: #3—THE KIDS

"Because my parents kept everything to themselves, I've always thought that it was a good thing to be completely honest and straightforward about everything with my own kids from their earliest years," says Brad, a friend we've known for years. "I told them their mother and I smoked marijuana, I let them know that their grandfather had been abusive to their grandmother. When they asked me, 'What happened to Uncle Pete?' I told them that he killed himself. I know that's tough to hear, but should I lie to them? Whenever they want to know something, I tell them the complete truth." Brad is like many parents. Honesty and full disclosure are values he wants to pass on to his children, and he tries to teach them through his own actions.

Serena, a mother of three, has another point of view. "I am a religious person and I believe in truth above all. But I also believe in protecting my children. There are some things I don't want them to know until they are ready to hear and to understand. For instance, my friend Jaynie is divorced, and she tells her preteen daughter, Sam, all about her boyfriends: when she sleeps with them, what they fight about, even what type of birth control they use. She also tells Sam things about what went wrong between her and her ex-husband. All the bad stuff. She doesn't seem to remember that her ex is Sam's father and it may be too hard for her to understand right now why they got divorced. It's very painful for Sam."

Brad and Jaynie represent one type of parent. They're forthright and up front with their kids. Serena and her husband carefully monitor what their children see and hear. Which is the best path for a parent to take?

Each of these parents will tell you they believe in strong values and good character. They believe in truth and honesty, but Brad and Jaynie may be taking these qualities too far for their children's good. As parents, maybe it's time for them to tighten up a bit.

Kids may interpret what a parent tells them in a very different way from how it was intended. Brad's fourth-grader doesn't have a grown-up's understanding of suicide and will most likely conjure up all kinds of terrifying images and ideas about his uncle's death. And does he need to know that his grandfather beat his grandmother? Perhaps it would be wiser to withhold such potentially disturbing information for a few years—all a nine-year-old needs to know is that his uncle has died. Jaynie's daughter, Sam, will learn the truth—good and bad—about her father as she matures. Is it necessary to burden her with stories about his philandering? Perhaps it would be more judicious to let her find out about him on her own. Ditto with her mother's boyfriends. Is it such a good idea to let a young daughter know about her mother's intimate sexual life before she's ready to handle that information?

We, too, believe in honesty and truth, in being forthright and direct. But we also believe that being a good parent means understanding what is best for a child or a young adult. So, hold on, Jayne and Brad, and tighten up with your kids. Remember, you have plenty of time later to be as loose as you want with them. And who knows? When you're older, you may want them to "tighten up" on what they share with you.

27

SHARE YOUR FEARS WITH YOURSELF AND YOUR COURAGE WITH OTHERS

We love these Magic Words, which were spoken by a true hero: Franklin D. Miller. In addition to the Medal of Honor, Mr. Miller, who died recently, was awarded the Silver Star, two Bronze Stars, the Air Medal, and six Purple Hearts in four years of active duty in Vietnam. He considered himself an ordinary guy who was able, at an extraordinary moment in his life, to push his fears into the background and do the things he had to do.

Mr. Miller, born in Elizabeth City, North Carolina, first went to Vietnam in 1966. He started out as an infantryman with the First Cavalry Division. After two years he transferred to the Green Berets. After a promotion to staff sergeant, he was assigned to a unit that led patrols into Laos and Cambodia, seeking intelligence on North Vietnamese troop movements.

Sergeant Miller was leading a seven-man patrol on January 5, 1970, when a booby trap injured five of his men. A North Vietnamese unit nearby was alerted by the explosion and attacked Miller's patrol. The attack continued through the day. During the ensuing firefight, Sergeant Miller was shot in the chest.

"I felt like I was being drowned," he recalled in an interview. He was about to panic, when he had "something of a religious experience." The image of his sergeant from basic training came to him. This man, Sergeant Roy Bumgarner, was regarded by Miller and many others as a "Superman" soldier. "It was like Sergeant Bumgarner was right there, saying 'Calm down, otherwise you'll scare yourself into shock.' I tried to calm down and think what I had to do."

What Franklin Miller did was repel two attacks, firing from a solitary exposed position, after an evacuation helicopter had been driven off by enemy fire. Miller was the only member of his patrol able to keep fighting. Finally, that night, with Miller almost out of ammunition, another helicopter was able to evacuate him and the other two soldiers still alive out of the area. Sergeant Miller received the Medal of Honor from President Nixon on June 15, 1971.

Franklin Miller occasionally spoke to Green Beret trainees. His credo: "Share your fears with yourself and your courage with others. You will inspire people to do things that are incredible." Who can disagree with that?

28

CLARITY TOMORROW
(OR THE NEXT DAY)

Valerie is Howard's close friend. A couple of years ago she was a highly successful stockbroker with an established firm, making tons of money. She was thrilled when she was transferred from New York to Silicon Valley. As a single woman she'd not only meet the legions of unattached Internet millionaires and be able to improve her golf, she'd get to know firsthand many of the companies she was recommending to her clients. Turned out the timing couldn't have been worse. Almost from the minute she moved into the luxurious home that she bought with a large mortgage, the market began to soften and then it tanked. She was laid off with no mercy (and no money). A job offer that intrigued her came her way, but the terms were stiff— she would have to take a demotion both emotionally and financially.

The company was prepared to negotiate with her, and Valerie, thinking it would take a few hours to reach a favorable agreement, hired a lawyer to help. The negotiations extended over days, then into an agonizing week, then two, and finally, in the third week, they reached a point where the parties believed that one last meeting would resolve all the outstanding issues.

On a Monday morning at 9:15, the gaggle of gray-suited lawyers and their clients met in a book-lined conference room to settle the final details. Valerie listened to the attorneys as they began to wrap up, and felt her gut begin to turn on itself. The terms were tough, and, because money was a big issue, she had agreed to many things that she knew she would resent in the future. Did she really want to do this? Was this the way she wanted to live her life? Could she live with these conditions?

The lawyers nodded their heads, shook hands over the table, and agreed that the final contract would be drawn up right away, with both their clients signing immediately. Valerie dearly needed the money in order to keep her house (and pay her steep legal fees). During the negotiations, she had come to dislike the company she was dealing with and wondered if she could ever succeed in doing the job she was being offered. The more Valerie thought about the terms of the agreement and the more she considered her own financial state, the more distressed she became. How could she sign a contract that made her feel like an indentured servant? Could she ever find something else to keep her from bankruptcy court? She needed the job but hated the deal.

Valerie had been keeping Howard posted on the twists and turns of the situation. After she left the lawyers that Monday morning, she called him and reported on the final details.

"I don't know what to do," she told him. "I am truly a wreck about this. You're the one with the magic words, do you have any for me?"

"Clarity tomorrow," Howard replied without missing a beat. Then he added, *"or the next day."*

Those wise words are Howard's version of the old adage "sleep on it." Twenty-four hours really can bring an entirely new perspective on a problem. Ned Rorem, Stravinsky's biographer, tells how the master, when unable to solve a musical conundrum, would simply WAIT. Stravinsky inevitably found the creative solution if he gave it enough time.

Valerie didn't have the luxury of an open-ended time frame. She had to make a decision to sign the papers or not but she determined to chill until the next day to see what she thought of the situation. She took in an afternoon movie, came home, watched TV, and finally fell asleep.

The next morning Valerie indeed had a fresh view. She realized she could wait a few more days before committing to the deal. They can hold off, she told herself—after all, they took almost a month to negotiate this, a bit more time will not make a any difference. The realization that she had a little breathing space in which to think buoyed her spirits and freed her mind.

Two days later Valerie called her lawyer and explained that during all the sturm and drang of the negotiations she'd come to believe that this company was not a good place to work and that she had decided not to take the job. She told him she was uncomfortable with the executives who would be her peers, and she believed that she wouldn't fit into their corporate culture. It would only be a matter of time before she left—or they wanted her to leave. She told him to exit the situation on her behalf as smoothly as possible and hung up.

How would she pay the mortgage and the bills? This is what she told herself:

1. She could always sell the house and move to a rental if she had to.

2. Bills could be paid in installments.

3. She would get another job, if not in California then back in New York.

To put it simply, when she took some time to regain her perspective and become clear on things, Valerie's faith in herself was restored, and she could see that she would survive this crisis.

The same kind of painful and protracted discussions that Valerie was involved in can occur with a divorce or separation, but the anguish, the grief, and the complexity are far, far greater. Even in the direst situations, "Clarity Tomorrow (or the Next Day)" really does work magic. Giving yourself 24 hours or more allows you time and space to let your unconscious mind think for you. Your own deepest self is where your best instincts are. When you wait for clarity tomorrow, you're permitting those instincts to surface, and they'll offer you a new perspective from which to make judgments and decisions.

As we went to press, Valerie had decided to withdraw some of her savings to pay for her living expenses, and to take a three-month hiatus to figure out what she wants out of life. She's looking forward to her next step, and she's sure she'll land on her feet. We're absolutely certain of it.

29

OF ALL THE MANY VOICES, LISTEN TO THE NEAREST ONE— YOURS

There are many people who know us well. Obviously, there's our parents (though sometimes, particularly when we were in our teens, we thought they didn't have a clue). Our brothers and sisters have some idea who we are. Add to that close friends and people we've worked with for a long time. Are we leaving anyone out? Probably. What unites all these people, aside from the fact that they love us, is that from time to time— or even all the time—they're giving us advice. The question is, how closely should we listen to them?

"It took me a while to figure out what paths were right for me," Betty, a friend from Tampa, told us a while back. "I always felt lucky that so many people cared about me. From early on I was showered with advice and directions. What school should I go to? What should I major in? Was this fellow, or that one, right for me? Is this the right area to live in? Most of their advice was given with my best interests at heart. I always felt obligated to place all this well-intentioned advice on the front burner. This led to decisions that weren't bad, but they weren't good, either. They simply weren't mine. I thanked God for the caring words of family and friends over all those years, but I finally realized that unless you give primacy to your own inner voice, you're nowhere.

"Why? They all thought they knew me, but they didn't know me nearly as well as I knew myself. Then there's my intuition—a pretty important part of me that others can only dimly appreciate. I still reach out for advice and counsel. It's an important part of the process for making major decisions. But I always listen more closely to my own voice. It knows me best.

"Recently, I received a job offer in Cincinnati. It was a terrific opportunity. Of course, I didn't know anyone there. I'd be away from family and friends. Not forever, but at least for a couple of years. I'd be giving up a great apartment. I had just started to see a guy, Jed, who I liked a lot. My chorus of advisors and supporters all weighed in. Their unanimous decision: don't take the job. Yes, it sounds terrific, they said, but it's too big a change. What if you don't like it, or, even worse, what if they don't like you? I listened to them carefully. Then I made my decision. I took the job. Jed decided that he wanted to be with me, so he found a job there, too. We've made a lot of friends, and a few months ago Jed and I got engaged. And you know what? My inner voice said quite clearly that Jed was the man for me."

Your family and friends have your best interests at heart, and often their advice is right on the money. But not always. Listen to them and weigh what they say closely, and then pay attention to the voice inside you. It will advise you in ways that no outsider can.

30

GET YOUR EGO OUT OF IT!

We were at a new friend's house one night, and he asked us to help him make some drinks in the kitchen. On the counter where he set down an unopened bottle of wine was a stack of personal papers with his pay stub on top. He could have easily removed the papers, but he didn't. Why? because he wanted us to see the numbers. He knew that he made much more than we did. He was doing some serious bragging, but secretly we thanked him because we immediately knew what kind of person he was. He needed to prove he was bigger and better than anyone else—and that's not what friendships are made of. All kinds of wars have been caused by egos. Worldwide conflagrations. Domestic combat. Professional battles. Personal skirmishes like the one above. And usually, at the root of it all is what we call "a hungry ego."

Every ego needs to be fed and nourished. Egos thrive on admiration, appreciation, and recognition. That's how they develop self-worth and self-esteem, those essential elements to get through life.

Examine a scrawny, skinny ego. For whatever reasons, it did not grow properly. There were probably parents who didn't supply it with enough love, and it matured into an emaciated thing, screaming for sustenance and demanding nourishment from everyone who comes its way. Now observe a nice, plump, healthy ego. It was nurtured by parents, provided with the all-important emotional goodies—love and attention. This ego enjoys reserves of confidence and self-reliance and quickly bounces back from any of life's insults it endures.

Most egos fall somewhere on a broad scale between the hefty and the starving, but all of us encounter circumstances where our ego butts in and causes difficulties. Our new friend's calculated gesture—leaving his pay stub on the counter—was a tip-off to his personality problem. His tip-off was a silent one, but there are words and phrases that indicate when someone's ego—yours or another person's—is getting in the way. Here are some you'll come across:

"You'd better back down on that."

"You're insulting me."

"My car [house, boat, bank account, wife or husband] is bigger and better than yours."

"Don't hand me that kind of treatment."

"I'm running this meeting."

"I'll never speak to him/her again."

"How dare he?"

"Who does she think she is?"

When you hear words to this effect, remember it's an ego that's speaking—a small ego that needs to make itself bigger at someone else's expense. So what if your neighbor's lawn is a brighter green, his Jaguar a sexier machine, his bank account higher, his private parts bigger. So what if your co-worker is prettier, smarter, and has a "ten" body or the hunkiest boyfriend in town? Does it mean you're less of a person, that you're unimportant, insignificant? Absolutely, positively not! If you have a healthy self-image and a good ration of self-esteem, you know you are valued and loved for the special, unique person that you are, and you're able to deal with almost any situation in a reasonable, mature way.

But now let's suppose someone else's ego leads them to get "in your face," and your own ego takes the bait. Save yourself a confrontation, as well as anguish, anger, bitterness, hatred—all of those emotions that poison the soul. Tell yourself:

GET YOUR EGO OUT OF IT!

That's what we did when we spied that pay stub. We didn't feel jealous or resentful because we knew we were doing just fine professionally and didn't need to make a big deal out of it or get into competition with the guy.

We first heard "Get Your Ego Out of It!" from the eminent New York psychiatrist Dr. John Train. He had the phrase needlepointed on a pillow on a chair in his office. He's the one who made us understand how essential that concept is, and we engraved those Magic Words in our minds and have thanked him every day since.

31

IF I DON'T START,
I DON'T HAVE A PROBLEM

Betcha can't eat just one: that old potato chip commercial definitely hits a very deep nerve. Think Ben & Jerry's, M&M's, whipped cream, french fries, triple chocolate-chip cookies... even pickles.

Jeri, a newspaper reporter, was working on an important investigative piece on a labor racketeering project. Since she was on a tight deadline, she found herself getting takeout lunches from the gourmet shop next door to her office. For the first week she stuck to her usual turkey sandwich or tuna-from-a-can with Diet Dr Pepper, but then she spied a row of large round glass self-service containers of nuts and dried fruits behind the deli area. Knowing she had a major weakness for unsalted cashews, she stayed away. But one day, just as a special treat, she scooped a handful of jumbo nuts into a plastic bag. The next day she was back, snapping up some more.

A week later, she was eating cashews for afternoon snacks and popping a few on the subway ride home. Two months passed, and she'd gained seven pounds plus a couple more from overdosing on morning Danish and wolfing down chunks of Taleggio cheese with an evening glass of wine.

We told her about Dr. Stephen Gullo, a well-known weight-control expert who would be able to help her quit the cashew habit. She made an appointment with him for the following week.

Jeri's problem is a common one. Many of us, according to Dr. Gullo, have "trigger foods" that activate a "can't-resist" process. Potato chips are a great example. Ice cream, bread, cake, and cookies are all culprits, as is almost anything that contains chocolate. How do you stop the process? Dr. Gullo prescribes these magic words:

If I don't start, I don't have a problem.

Jeri wrote them on a piece of paper, which she Scotch-taped to her change purse. If she surrendered to her urges and loaded up on cashews, when she reached the checkout counter she'd give them back to the cashier. If she was at a party and a bowl of nuts came into view, Dr. Gullo advised that she move out of range immediately and repeat the magic words to herself. At the end of three weeks Jeri had shed half a dozen pounds and was well on her way to zipping up her Levi's again.

Dr. Gullo's magic words also work for problems that don't involve food. For instance, it's easy to start complaining in to-day's stressful employment climate—the boss is inaccessible, the hours are excruciating, the pay is unfair, blah, blah, blah. Complaining begets more complaining and inevitably the boss finds out who started the griping, so it's bad for the complainer—and for general morale. A lot of people have a tendency to air griev-ances around the water cooler. If you're one of those who sets up a negative situation, do yourself a favor and say "If I don't start . . . ," and you and your co-workers will steer clear of a common problem.

Nagging is another prime area where "If I don't start" has a positive effect. Unfortunately, women have been stereotyped as naggers, though in many cases they nag for very good reasons. Men nag too. We think it can easily be stopped by changing the magic words slightly, to "If I don't start, WE don't have a problem."

From nachos to nagging, cashews to complaining, the best approach to stopping something you shouldn't be doing is not starting in the first place.

32

WHEN IS SAYING "I'M SORRY" NOT ENOUGH?

The answer is easy: for serious issues, it's never enough to say only "I'm sorry."

When your shopping cart brushes against someone else's as you make your way down the aisle of the supermarket, "I'm sorry" is perfectly adequate. Ditto when you accidentally kick some sand onto someone's blanket at the beach (though be sure to help clean it off). But save those two words for life's minor blunders.

A while back, Kristin, who's a court reporter in Baton Rouge, told us a story that underlined the inadequacy of those words:

"The problem with saying, 'I'm sorry,' is that a lot of people just end it there. Saying it should just be the beginning. A couple of years ago I had a boyfriend named Ronnie. We were together for a year. Ronnie was lots of fun to be with. He had a sweet nature and was generally pretty considerate. His downside, and it was a big one, was an amazing lack of responsibility. He would regularly lose my keys, show up late—or sometimes not at all—for dinner dates, and make promises that he only occasionally kept. But Ronnie was fun.

"An important part of my life at that time was my dog. His

name was 'This and That.' Actually, I called him just 'That.' The name came from his breeding. I found him in a pound. He was midsized, brown with a spattering of white around his muzzle. He was adorable. When people would ask me what his breed was, I would say he was made up of this and that. I loved That. Maybe a lot of it had to do with his loving me. Unconditionally.

"One day I had to spend some time helping a friend who had just gotten out of the hospital. I asked Ronnie to go to my place and feed That. Simple, right? When he got there, he went to the living room and started watching a football game. Of course, he also forgot to close the back door after he entered. Guess what? My dog hightailed it out the door. When I got home, Ronnie was still watching the game. The door was still wide open. That was gone.

'Gee, I'm really sorry, Kris,' he said, his eyes still on the football game.

'That's not enough, Ronnie. Not nearly enough. Why aren't you out looking for That?'

"Well, he finally got his butt off the sofa and out to the street. He kept muttering, 'I'm sorry,' but he only looked half-heartedly. I could see he just wanted to go back and watch the damn football game. And did he help me make up posters to tack onto telephone poles the next day? You know the answer to that. Someone finally returned my dog about a week later. By then I knew that I wanted Ronnie out of my life permanently."

Never forget, for serious mistakes or errors in judgment, "I'm sorry" is just the start. We could write a whole book on all the things those two words don't cover. Our rule is simple: when you say "I'm sorry" in a situation where more is needed, skip those words and get busy doing the "more."

33

I'M GOING TO LEND
MYSELF A HELPING HAND

SHE: I've worked hard all my life to get to the top. And it's not so great up here. I'm thinking seriously of quitting and looking for a job in a flower shop.

SELF: You're at the pinnacle of success, your name's in boldface in the gossip columns, you get the best restaurant tables, you hobnob with CEOs and movie stars, you can buy almost anything you want. How bad can it be?

SHE: My CEO is an egomaniac and a pathological liar, my staff whines like pathetic babies. If I go on a three-day vacation, all of them are yammering at me 24/7.

SELF: Isn't this the price you pay for earning The Big Bucks?

SHE: No question that I like the money and the power—

SELF: Remember that statement—

SHE: But the pressure is becoming unbearable. I've turned the business around, and no one around this place has even bothered to notice what I've achieved. I'm tired right down to my soul.

SELF: Ah, now I get it. You're feeling sorry for yourself because nobody's patting you on the back to tell you how great you are.

SHE: Well, they could at least acknowledge all that I've done and how fast I've done it.

SELF: Careful, you're turning into a whiner yourself.

SHE: It's more like I can't handle it anymore. After all I'm only one person doing all this work, with all the responsibility—

SELF: Plus the lovely smackeroos . . . the clothing allowance . . . AND a fancy car service . . .

SHE: I'm gonna quit. This time I really mean it. I can't keep going at this pace.

SELF: Yeah, you do need a vacation, but you also need some help.

SHE: And where, my friend, do you think I'll find it? A shrink? I've seen one. I'm mentally as healthy as anyone. A boyfriend? When do I have time? And most of the men out there—

SELF: Kvetching again. At your professional level and at your age, nobody is going to hand out praise and compliments to you. With that salary and that title, you're *expected* to produce. You're only doing your job. Why should anybody go into raptures over you?

SHE: We all need to know we're appreciated. We need someone to recognize that.

SELF: But your recognition comes from the fact that they pay you and keep you in that beautiful office and those beautiful Armanis. What you need to do is *lend yourself a helping hand.*

SHE: Maybe you're on to something. It wouldn't hurt to give myself some congratulations, tell myself I've turned things around and I'm doing a great job—since no one else will. I'll feel better if I give myself some pats on the back once in a while.

We really don't feel a bit sorry for the "She" in this inner dialogue. It was her choice to follow that career path, it was her decision to cash those sweet paychecks every month. She is wiped out, not from working sixteen-hour days, but because she needs acknowledgment and applause for what she's accomplished. Once "She" starts to lend herself a helping hand by giving herself the ego nourishment and accolades she needs, she'll begin to genuinely enjoy the power and status of the position that enticed and excited her in the first place.

Certain things are required of adults: We're expected to do our jobs, rally round aging parents, deal with the terminal illness of a loved one, and cope with situations that we never thought life had in store for us. You have the choice of scrapping all your responsibilities and becoming a hermit, but in our book, being a grown-up calls for facing the music. Sometimes you're all alone in tight straits, and it's at these moments that you need to lend yourself a helping hand and tell yourself that you're giving it your best shot and you're doing just fine under the circumstances. You may never have thought about it, or you may have forgotten that you possess deep reserves of personal power and emotional stamina. These are the coffers to tap when you need extra strength to get you through. That helping hand you lend yourself holds the key to a less complicated, more satisfying life.

34

WIND IT, DON'T TURN IT BACK

Every morning at precisely 4:21—not a nanosecond earlier or later—Tim woke up with his brain racing... That house on Roxbury Lane, he could have stretched to buy it and now it's worth double what he would have paid... He should have seen the doctor when Katie told him the mole on his back looked suspicious. When he finally got to it, the spot had turned into a nasty skin cancer... They should have sent their daughter to private school. Tried to land a scholarship for her. She would have been a much stronger reader now... Maybe they should have moved back to Berkeley, where it was easier to raise a child... It probably would have been better if they'd had another kid.

On and on went the recriminations, the rehashing, the scrutinizing of each event, each twist and turn of Tim's existence, starting every morning at precisely 4:21. Tim was so desperate to stop waking up and replaying every fear in his life that he dreaded going to bed at night. He tried sleeping pills, warm milk, hot baths, and soothing music. He bought a machine that spewed white noise, studied yoga, swallowed double doses of Excedrin PM, threw back a couple of shots of Jack

Daniel's, and finally smoked some pot, but nothing could lull him back to sleep. . . .

Helen C. is an 82-year-old grandmother, a great talker and a connoisseur of fascinating stories. A natural chronicler, she used to spin riveting yarns about her life and times. Both family and friends loved to hear her tales. As she grew older she became even more long-winded and more attached to the past. She'd talk about her dear mother and what a wonderful cook she was, about the untimely death of her father when she was six; she'd share endless anecdotes about her seven brothers and sisters. The stories became repetitive, and her children and grandkids grew bored and restless. Then Helen would begin reminiscing about how she was ripped off by her accountant four years ago, what things cost in the old days, and how she just couldn't understand what was happening with kids and sex and violence and the astronomically high prices of eggs and bread and oleomargarine . . .

The past was taking over Helen's life, the same thing was happening to Tim. Even though they were thirty years apart in age, both were suffering from the slings and arrows of their personal histories. Helen's behavior was a turnoff to everyone who came in contact with her, and Tim was a physical and emotional wreck from loss of sleep.

They both needed to use these magic words: *wind it, don't turn it back.*

You can't turn back the clock, but you can wind it up and start it ticking again. Tim, start ruminating on the good stuff: your adorable daughter, the freedom of being an artist, the garden that you love. You can still find a good real-estate deal. You can still move to the West Coast if you really want to. Your career may have taken some wrong turns, but you can still make smart decisions and start moving on a different track. We bet if you go to sleep ruminating this new way, chances are that after a night or two you'll sleep right through till eight o'clock every morning.

And Helen, you're a hearty 82 and you have every right to be nostalgic, but don't mire your family in the old times when they're sick and tired of hearing about them. Don't turn the clock back, wind it up, so that every day it will tick with interesting stories that are happening to you right now: your conversation with the long-distance information operator and how you found out that she's one of fifteen children (!) and has the best recipe on earth for Swedish cookies, your search for the perfect present for your great-grandchild, the latest book you've been reading. Your fabulous talent as a raconteur can make all these everyday happenings into events, and you'll regain your audience—and probably even expand it.

So Tim and Helen, and all of you who are much too attached to the past, don't turn back the clock. Better yet buy a digital one with big red numbers, and it will remind you to stay firmly in the present where you belong.

35

"I-NEED"S

You know that you need food, shelter, sex, sunlight, money—
and a few other big, indispensable things. But when was the
last time you thought about the small stuff that helps you get
through a day or a week—a little luxury, or an experience that
lights up your life, gives you pleasure, makes it all a bit more
worthwhile. Recently, each of us did just that, and we came up
with lists of "I-need"s.

HOWARD'S "I-NEED"S:

A glass of freshly squeezed orange juice

Really polished shoes

A clean handkerchief

Two books at my bedside

A song by Ella Fitzgerald to start the day

A chilled glass of white wine before dinner

ALEXANDRA'S "I-NEED"S:

Morning coffee in a pretty cup, preferably in bed

Nice soap

Ten minutes to transition from work to private life

Clean surfaces, i.e., no clutter around me

Fresh, brightly colored flowers whenever possible

"I-need"s rarely cost much—if anything—in monetary terms, but they mean a great deal to all of us. The easy delights of a hot bath with a fragrant candle, watching Monday-night football, a gleaming just-washed car, an ironed handkerchief— each can make someone's day a bit more pleasant. They provide small moments of contentment that help maintain your sanity when the world is too much with you. Take a minute to improve your mental health by listing your own "I-need"s. And do you know what your mate's "I-need"s are? When was the last time you squeezed some fresh OJ for him or her? Kept the kids out of the bedroom for a few minutes while he or she sipped some coffee and sank back into the pillows? Didn't turn on the TV for twenty-four hours? When was the last time you gave your love—or yourself—a single, perfect rose?

36

IF YOU WANT TO GAIN CONTROL,
YOU HAVE TO GIVE UP CONTROL

Sounds like a contradiction, doesn't it? But it's not. Over the years we've mostly used these Magic Words at work, but they can apply in a variety of situations.

"Do you have any problem letting your doctor administer your annual physical?" asks our friend Cheryl. "I don't. I also have my dry cleaner take care of my clothes. And when I need a tune-up on my Volvo, I don't think twice about having Art at the garage do it. What am I driving at here? A lesson I learned from my first boss, Barney W. He was sales director of the company, a pretty important job, and I was hired to be one of four regional sales managers. It was my first position out of business school. I liked him immediately. Barney was fair minded, he was a hard worker, and he had a good sense of humor and never lost his temper. But he had a problem as a manager, and it was a big one. No matter how highly he thought of you and your abilities, he had the urge to do your job. It was maddening. He couldn't cede responsibility on anything. I had sixteen salespeople reporting to me, but Barney had to look over and sign all their expense accounts. When we had our quarterly sales meeting, Barney had to check the audiovisual equipment even though he wasn't making any presentations. He also had to approve the menus for the meals we ate at the hotel!

"At first I found his behavior funny. 'It's just my Mother Hen personality,' he would say to me. But after a while it started to drive me crazy. 'Barney, you have a big enough job without trying to do mine,' I would tell him. He'd smile and tell me that he just wanted to make my life easier. But all he was doing was stopping me from doing my job properly. I left the company after a year for a position that paid less but really gave me the responsibility I was seeking—a job where I could demonstrate all my abilities. Some years later I ran into Barney in an airport. He was no longer the sales director.... He had been demoted to sales manager."

The reality in life is that we control very few of the events that swirl around us. If you run a large corporation or manage a Little League team, you face the same problem every day: you must depend on others. By obsessively trying to control everything, you'll be missing out on what we all need: the help of others. We have to give up some control every day if we want to successfully make our way ahead. We don't think for a second when we get on a plane that we must sit next to the pilot and tell him how to take off, do we? Same goes for our trips to the dentist. When he says, 'Say, Ahh,' we say, 'Ahh'. If you have people working for you, they were hired for one reason: their ability. If you want to accomplish big things, you have to let others do big things, too. And who wants to be called a control freak, anyway?

37

HEY, IT'S ONLY THE
SECOND INNING

Reminiscent of Yogi Berra's most famous Yogi-ism, "It ain't over till it's over," these Magic Words immediately struck a chord with us when our friend William passed them on a few years back. William, who's a dentist, is in his mid-forties. He's married, with two children in high school. He's a friendly, kind man, the type that people like to be around. The one character trait that troubles him and his wife, Amy, is that he's a chronic worrier.

"I guess I've worried about things, big and small, ever since I was a little kid. My brother and sister used to tease me when I worried about my Halloween costume, social studies paper, or whether or not I would start on my Little League team. I don't want to portray myself as a basket case who's stuck in permanent gridlock from worrying. It's not that bad. But it's not good, either. I've tried a lot of things, including seeing an analyst, over the years. But the thing I keep coming back to is something my dad would always say to me when I was a kid: 'Hey, it's only the second inning.' "

"It took me a while to understand what he was getting at with those words. To me it means that things are never as bad as they seem. There's still time ahead for you to get on top of the situation. Time to change things, time to set a new course. Maybe it isn't really the second inning in real life, but it's not the bottom of the ninth either. We'll all eventually reach the last inning, but, hopefully, that's way down the line."

These Magic Words can be used for all types of stress, any time you feel inundated by the chores and burdens of life.

Let's say you're giving an important dinner party—meeting your boyfriend's parents for the first time or having the new boss and his wife over. You serve an elaborate dish that you never tried before, but it looked good in the magazine. Of course, the dish is a disaster, and your guests are due to arrive in an hour. What do you do? Try saying the Magic Words, and your anxiety will ratchet down and a solution will appear. You'll remember that you make a great linguine with puttanesca sauce, which everybody loves and which takes less than an hour. So what if it isn't fancy? It's good.

38

IF LIONS ARE SUCH MESSY EATERS, WHY DO I ALWAYS WANT THE LION'S SHARE?

"I've always considered myself a generous, thoughtful person," Ginger told us. "I don't mean the gifts I give at Christmastime (which, by the way, both of us know are terrific). Or remembering the birthdays of all my friends and everyone in my family. If I hear that a friend needs anything, from a loan to a baby-sitter, I'm there for them, and I pride myself on it. So I was real surprised by what my brother, Tom, said to me recently. We were going to a movie, and while Tom was paying for the taxi, I dashed ahead to get the tickets. Then I met Tom at the concession counter, where he was buying popcorn.

" 'You know, Ginger, you haven't changed one iota since you were a kid.'

" 'What do you mean?' I asked him.

" 'You just artfully jumped the line and got ahead of a quartet of ladies who saw eighty at least a few years ago.'

"For once I didn't have an answer. It was a splash of *very* cold water in my face to hear Tom say that. For a moment my mind flashed back to the scene a few moments ago. I saw myself sneak ahead of the four elderly people. Why did I do that? I realized I had always done things like that.

" 'I guess it's not a great trait,' I finally admitted.

" 'That's one way to phrase it. You know, it's become a joke with all your friends. "Where's Ginger?" "Why, at the head of the line, of course." It doesn't bother them much since it's not them you're cutting in front of. But the people you've slid, pushed, or squeezed your way past over the years might feel differently.' "

We all are able to spot greed in others without much difficulty. The person who takes the last cookie from the plate is pretty easy to target. What about the person who races around you to get the only parking spot on the block? That's obvious, too, though in New York who can blame them? Other types of greedy behavior abound, and some are a little less easy to notice. But have you looked at yourself lately? Try this exercise: It's raining a bit. Not a downpour, but more than a sprinkle. You want to hail a taxi. But, damn it, there's a woman waving her hand for a cab ahead of you. Would you walk down the street a block or so to get ahead of the woman? Be honest, now. You're probably walking already. You might stroll far enough away that she won't even see you when the taxi stops and you get inside. That's what we sometimes do. We call this type of thing *elegant greed*. You know something? It's not nice, and we're working to cut it down in our lives. (We did not say *out* because we're realists.) Generous behavior is appreciated by everyone. And strangely enough, just *not* being greedy will make lots of people think you a generous person. So walk back to that woman and wait for her to get her taxi. There'll be another one coming along for you in a few minutes. Constantly reaching out for the Lion's Share, no matter how elegantly, isn't a flattering trait. Plus, lions have to work so hard to get the lion's share, and watching them eat is not a pretty sight.

39

I'M NOT LONELY WHEN I'M ALONE

The Beatles sang of all the lonely people—and the planet is full of them. Men and women who dread isolation and separateness and who will do almost anything to avoid being alone. We know a man who, during the years before he married, went through a string of semi-serious relationships. If someone he was dating was unavailable for the evening, he'd go on the prowl and end up in another woman's bedroom. He owns up to several hundred one-night stands. He told us he simply could not stand being alone. And we've read about women—and seen them on TV—who can match his bed-hopping record.

Whether it takes the form of sleeping around or inviting themselves to parties, or loitering long after the party's over, lots of people cannot tolerate loneliness. They will do almost anything—including having sex with strangers—to alleviate the remoteness they experience, even for a little while.

We have an acquaintance who told us that she feels so desperate that she's going to hire a live-in housekeeper, even though she will have to make many sacrifices to afford one. "She won't be a friend or someone I can talk to," this woman says, "but at least I know I won't be alone."

You don't even have to be alone to be lonely. A young

woman in her freshman year in college told us that she has two roommates and still she feels pangs of loneliness. A long-married man says he feels most lonely when he's home with his wife on a Saturday night and their teenage daughter is out on a date. And surely you've heard of people—you might be one of them—who suffer from loneliness at a cocktail party or a family get-together.

As clichéd as this sounds, you're never really alone, because there's always one fascinating individual who's with you—body and soul—every nanosecond of your life. Of course, we are talking about you yourself.

There are times in life when we all need companionship. But if loneliness is something you're dealing with every day—whether you're alone or not—keep the following in mind. You are a human being unlike any other. Get to know the many aspects of this unique person—both positive and negative—and you'll find that there is no one as intriguing as you. Use your time alone to delve into the nooks and crannies of your remarkable psyche. You'll unearth dreams, fantasies, and desires you probably never knew you had. Step back from the fears and demons that haunt you and map out ways to demolish them. If being alone is something you think you really can't stand, face your fears head-on and take a weekend trip all by yourself. Once you begin to enjoy your own company and see what a fascinating character you truly are, you'll be off on a lifelong journey with a beguiling travel companion. If loneliness should ever hover on the horizon and begin to cloud your day, use these powerful Magic Words to destroy its thunder: "I'm Not Lonely When I'm Alone."

40

KEEP IN MOTION (OR K.I.M.)

K.I.M. is for those times in your life when you're not sure you're going to make it. For when you're practically out of your mind with anxiety. Or when you're experiencing the worst kind of grief.

Alice Goodwin, 35 years old, is married to a dairy farmer and has two daughters, Emma and Claire. One sunny day in June, Emma started the morning with a violent tantrum. Claire ate an unknown number of pennies, and it was Alice's turn to watch her best friend's two small girls as well as her own children. She absentmindedly stole a minute alone that turned into ten: time enough for a devastating accident to occur. Her friend's daughter, Lizzie, drowned in the farm's pond. . . . This is how Jane Hamilton's moving novel *A Map of the World* begins.

Alice's husband, a strong, quiet dairy farmer, saw her sliding into the blackest despair from grief and guilt but felt powerless to help her. When Alice couldn't get out of bed, when she had even stopped taking care of her children, he took her hand and said to her simply, "*. . . keep in motion. Say that to yourself.*"

The process of living can arouse rapture and awe. It can also bring grief, despair, anxiety, devastation. Being human means feeling intense emotions that may, at times, threaten to overwhelm you. Each of us feels and responds to deep emotions differently. Often we see a person spiral down into a paralysis brought on by grief or melancholy, as the fictional Alice Goodwin did. We retreat into ourselves, make no effort to take care of ourselves, to see friends, or to find someone who could help.

When a beloved family member dies, the period of deepest grief is usually delayed while the details of the death and funeral are taken care of. The *motions* of attending to formalities help to get you through. That is what Alice Goodwin's husband, Howard, meant when he told her to "keep in motion." Just going through the motions of day-to-day living—brushing one's teeth, brewing coffee, cooking, cleaning up—can help ameliorate even the bleakest feelings. Going through the motions gives you much-needed time to pull yourself back together after the hurricane of feelings that mark loss or grief.

It's not easy, we know. Keeping in motion requires control, and emotions don't like to be controlled. How, then, do you Keep in Motion when you want to be inert, when all you want to do is sleep for days or months—or forever?

In both our lives, when we have faced the worst, we have found that by repeating Keep in Motion as a mantra, we can rouse ourselves to move around, haul our bodies into the car, drag ourselves to work, do the grocery shopping, even push ourselves to mow the lawn. There must be a sound psychological explanation for why the repetition of the words works. Neither of us is aware of the reason, but that doesn't stop us from suggesting to friends who are enmeshed in heartbreaking split-ups, times of great loss, or devastating experiences, to repeat the Magic Words as often as possible. One day, you'll have gotten out of bed, eaten breakfast, gone to work—you'll be halfway through your day before you realize that for the first time in a long while, you didn't have to chant the words to do it.

We hope you never have to face the kind of desolation and hopelessness that the heroine of Jane Hamilton's novel did, but if you do have to cope with black feelings, K.I.M. can help. When you find yourself in very deep water, do you make your legs move to avoid drowning, or do you stop all activity and sink to the bottom? Whether you're literally drowning or drowning emotionally, your only choice is to "Keep in Motion."

41

I HAVE TO STOP GRIEVING FOR YOU NOW (BUT I'M NEVER GOING TO STOP LOVING YOU)

Everyone has suffered the loss of a beloved family member or friend. If you haven't, we're sorry to say it, but someday you will. The death of someone who's one of the numbers in the combination that unlocks your heart can leave a void that's like a black hole—it seems to pull all the joy in life out of you.

"My mother died suddenly when I was just thirty," our friend Emily told us. "She had been in seemingly perfect health. She had planned my thirtieth-birthday party and danced more than I did that night. When my father called me that Tuesday morning, I suddenly felt like I was four years old again.

"The funeral service and period of mourning afterward are still a blur to me. My family gathered close together, as if they were taking shelter from a storm. I don't know what would have happened to me if I hadn't had them with me at that time. My boyfriend, Herb, was a strong support and stayed by my side the whole time. My father handled it well, or, I guess, as well as anyone can who's lost the person they adored for over thirty-six years.

"Six months later I had slowly worked my way back from Mom's death to the land of the living, or I thought I had. I was involved with my work, went to movies and concerts with

Herb, had dinner with my father every week, and saw my friends.

"One night, while I was walking home with Herb after having dinner at a local Chinese restaurant, he stopped and put his hands on my shoulders.

" 'Em, you know I care for you a lot,' he said, and then I started to cry. Big, blubbery tears, a carwash of tears. He pulled me close, and after a while I was able to stop.

" 'I don't know what just got into me,' I started to explain to him.

" 'That's just what I wanted to talk to you about. It's your mother.'

" 'My mother?'

" 'Ellie was a great woman. I wish I had been able to spend more time with her. She was a real winner. But you have to stop mourning her. It's not what she would have wanted.'

" 'I don't understand.'

" 'You're going through your life like a sleepwalker, Em. There's nothing wrong with grieving for a wonderful person like your mother for a long time. That's the way it should be. But eventually you have to put it behind you and switch to re-membering that person in a different way. One defined not just by the weight of loss. A remembrance that's more about love.'

"Of course, at first I denied what Herb was telling me. I was a big girl and I was in charge of my life. I was fine. But in time I saw that he was right. I really was shuffling through my life. My eyes were open, but I didn't see much. Now when I think of my mother I smile, because I remember her for what she was: warm and funny and, in a special way, very much alive."

Some of us suffer from the loss of a loved one for a long, long time—sometimes far too long. The person you're grieving for wouldn't have wanted you to go through this for so long. What would they want? They'd want you to remember that truly funny thing that was said when the turkey was carved at that Thanksgiving dinner many years ago (the carving was atrocious but the meal was truly memorable). They'd want you to recall all the hugs, kisses, loving looks across the room, and time spent sitting on the couch late at night when no words were ever required. Though grieving for someone is a necessary process, it has to end. Only when it's finally over can the best form of remembrance begin. And remember that the love you had for that person will stay with you for the rest of your life.

42

FUTURISTA

Hank and Janet live in New York City. Janet owns a small T-shirt boutique, and Hank is a novelist. The store is their main source of income, and Hank writes freelance articles that bring in money sporadically. They've been married about fifteen years, and although they live in a nice, sunny apartment on Manhattan's Upper West Side, they're citizens of another universe. Let us explain.

When they first met and fell in love, they had wonderful dreams for the years to come. Hank would be wildly successful. His books would be made into movies and make millions. Janet would become a power in the fashion world by designing cool T-shirts and hot jeans and setting up boutiques from coast to coast. Then she'd open a fabulous restaurant and produce Broadway shows. Their hopes and plans for the future were the centerpiece of their relationship.

The years went by, and Hank's first and second novels received mediocre reviews. Janet never developed her own designs and became timid about expansion, fearing that she wouldn't be able to find the right location for her stores, or the best people to manage them. But she kept thinking about the day she'd see her clothes featured in fashion spreads in

Vogue, and the doors to her bistro opening wide to the in-crowd. Hank wrote a third novel that didn't get published, but he kept dreaming of hitting it big with his next one, and with the incredible movie deal and TV series that would come out of it.

Hank and Janet are not close friends of ours—for a specific reason. We knew them well and enjoyed their company years ago, but as time went by, we grew weary of all that focus on a future that never materialized. They never joined us in the here and now. Sure, we all have hopes and dreams—life would be pretty empty without them—but by living for tomorrow you're wrecking today. It's this hour, this minute, this second that counts. If you're thinking about what's going to happen, you're not paying attention to what *is* happening, and, what's worse, you're not doing anything to claim that future. How can you enjoy the taste of an over-the-top fudge sundae, or a baby's grin, when you're living in another realm—the world-of-what's-to-come. We came up with a Magic Word for Hank and Janet—*futuristas.* Futuristas can be fine for an evening or two but not for a steady friendship. No one knows what tomorrow will bring. The only way to enjoy the sweetness and romance of life is to embrace every minute as it happens.

43

THE GIFT OF WORRY

The rumor spread through the office like a brushfire. A new headquarters was being built in Oregon, and the staff would be relocating. The news made Bill completely miserable. From the minute he heard it, he couldn't sleep, couldn't concentrate, couldn't get through the day without huge hailstones of worry pelting him from every angle.

Bill was a natural-born worrier. He fretted about his prize roses, he fussed over his phone bills, he was concerned about road conditions, the weather pattern . . . but when big issues like health and money problems loomed, he went into worry overkill. The office move was a major example. Omigod, what did it mean? Could he sell his house for what it was worth? The children would be wrenched from their schools, could they adapt? Would his wife find another job? There was no end to the worries that beset him once he'd heard the relocation rumor. Fortunately, Bill's wife didn't agonize the way he did. In fact, she'd learned to adjust to his qualms by helping to solve them. As soon as she recognized the symptoms of his extravagant worrying, she'd say, "Bill, it's time to sit down and deal with the situation or you'll make yourself—and me—

crazy. Ask yourself: is there anything we can do about this office problem? If the answer is no, quit worrying and try to relax. If the answer's yes, something can be done, then do it!"

Even though Bill was a worrier he genuinely hated worrying and the anguish it caused him, so that night he sat in his easy chair with a bottle of beer and thought about what his wife had said. Yes, he could do something. He could find out the facts. If the company was actually about to move, he himself had better get moving instead of just worrying. The very next morning he asked his boss whether the rumor was true. His boss confirmed that new headquarters were being constructed outside Portland but told him, "Your department is staying right here." The knot in Bill's gut dissolved and he realized he shouldn't have waited. He should have talked to his boss as soon as he heard about the move. He should have found out what was really going on instead of imagining what *might* happen and worrying about it.

Worrying gives many people a headache or heartburn. When you have a really bad case like Bill, it's possible to damage your health even further from loss of sleep, appetite, and perspective. But worrying can actually be a gift. Suppose you've been getting quite a few stomachaches. You can hope they'll just clear up or you can be concerned about them. If your worrying causes you to call your doctor for a checkup and he finds you have an ulcer, your worrying has been very helpful. If you just continue to circle the worry track and don't pick up the phone, your ulcer is going to develop into something far more nasty.

When you feel your stomach tighten and your mind begin to flutter around and around the same fear, ask yourself, "Is this the Gift of Worry?" If it is—if you can do something about whatever is bothering you—do it. If there's nothing you can do, you're indulging in wasteful worrying. Toss it into the worry compactor, so that it can be squeezed into a small package and kicked out of your life.

44

THINK, DON'T FEEL

The experts you see on television and read about in newspapers and magazines often say, "Let your feelings out, don't hide them, it's not healthy." We want to offer some very different advice, *Think, don't feel.*

There are times when emotions clobber you from every angle—you're so flooded with feelings that you find yourself in gridlock, unable to think straight or act reasonably. One woman we know, Pat, could have used these Magic Words when she was swamped with emotions and started to cry in a public elevator.

Pat was on her way to an important interview on the forty-ninth floor of an office building in Chicago. She wanted the job badly, had passed muster with the human resources department and a senior vice president, and was now about to meet the woman who, she hoped, would be her boss. Muzak was playing when she entered the elevator. One tune was sliding seamlessly into the next, and as Pat heard the opening notes to "Someone to Watch over Me" she couldn't help herself, she started to cry.

Pat had recently signed the final papers in a nasty divorce, and she and her ex-husband had thought of this as "their song."

As she heard the melody, she saw herself dancing with Tim, body to body, spirit to spirit, on their first Christmas Eve, as snowflakes fell softly outside their window and stacks of presents glittered in the holiday lights.

"I absolutely *must* stop," she commanded herself, but the shut-off valves for her feelings didn't work. The tears kept coming. The elevator was nearing her floor, and she still couldn't get control of herself. When the receptionist asked whom she wanted to see, she asked for the ladies' room, where she blew her nose, swabbed away the mascara that had trickled down her cheeks, and tried to pull herself together to face the interview.

Therapists counsel that hiding or repressing feelings can be unhealthy and even dangerous. Opening up your feelings is fine in a professional's office or when you're with close friends and loved ones but just doesn't cut it when you need to project a rational, professional image.

A distinguished rabbi once counseled a distraught member of his congregation who needed to function at work after his wife's accidental death to "think, don't feel," and that person passed those Magic Words on to us.

If Pat had told herself to use her mind instead of letting her emotions run away with her—*think, Pat, don't feel*—she would have reached the forty-ninth floor in a much better state. The second she felt herself sinking into quicksand, this line of thinking about her ex-husband could have helped restore her equilibrium: Tim was a borderline alcoholic, he had cheated on her and lied to her, Pat couldn't trust him or depend on him— not a good basis for a marriage. Sure, they had their good times and memorable experiences, but he was not the guy for her. The act of thinking—one thought rationally followed by another—blots out the uninvited feelings and focuses the mind on the task at hand.

The good news about Pat is that she got the job. She didn't tell us how, but perhaps, as she was walking down the hall to the interview, she started to consider just how much she wanted to work there, what kind of salary she should ask for, what her co-workers would be like—perhaps she began to think, not feel—and that's how she really nailed the interview and landed the job.

45

DON'T PUNT ON THE FIRST DOWN

Even though the doctor walked into the examining room with a neutral expression on her face, Christy was certain that it was bad news, and the pounding of her heart was like nothing she'd ever felt before. "We see something on your mammogram," the doctor said in a gentle voice. "It's probably nothing, but I want to do an aspiration just to make sure. It's a simple procedure, nothing to be afraid of. Can you come in tomorrow?"

Christy nodded, unable to speak. To this day, she can't remember how she got dressed or how she left the office and drove home. By the time she called Dan, her boyfriend, she had already—in her mind—had a mastectomy, lost her hair to chemo, and died a horrible, painful death within the year.

Dan told Christy to meet him in ten minutes in a cafe next to his office. Over a couple of cappuccinos, he said, reasonably, "You don't know if you have cancer, Christy. It could even be a glitch in the film. The doctor herself said it was most likely nothing. An aspiration isn't even a serious biopsy. You've jumped all the way to a mastectomy—and even death, for God's sake—when you don't have all the facts. You've punted on the first down."

Christy was a dedicated Yankee fan—and had only the

dimmest idea of what Dan was talking about. So he explained briefly: You have four downs in football. Without getting too technical, punting is a play usually reserved for the fourth down. If you punt on the first down, you're giving up all your opportunities to score or gain ground. "In a word," he said, giving her a huge bear hug, "punting on the first down is a panic reaction. And you're freaking out unnecessarily. You've jumped to conclusions, gone through all your options without even knowing what they are. Let's wait and see what happens tomorrow."

That night, Christy tried to sleep, but terrifying thoughts kept careening through her head. By morning she found she actually could control her racing mind by saying to herself, "Don't punt on the first down." Dan was with her when she had the simple procedure done. As the technician looked at the computer screen to assess the situation, Christy was anxious but not out of control. When they entered the doctor's office to hear the results, Christy repeated Dan's words to herself.

"Everything is fine," the doctor reported, "it was just a cyst. We've taken care of it. I'll see you for your regular checkup next year." Christy almost danced out of the office, while Dan, who was, naturally, also enormously relieved, just smiled to himself.

Dan's Magic Words could also have helped Todd and Annie, a couple we once met. They were told by a local carpenter who built some kitchen shelves for them that they had termites throughout their house. They pictured their home turning to dust and all the money they'd spent on renovations disappearing down the drain. Their neighbor, who overheard the conversation, advised Todd and Annie to put the house on the market immediately. So Annie called Todd's cousin, a real estate broker, confidentially told her about their problem, and asked her to prepare a listing. Instead of putting up a "For Sale" sign on their front lawn, the cousin insisted Todd and Annie hire a pest-control expert. Turned out the "termites" were harmless insects that could be exterminated with a morning's work.

There are many situations where people are terrified or fall to pieces for no real reason, and they come to a desperate conclusion or take a last-ditch action. They may listen to one person's opinion and never seek a second. They don't think through consequences or investigate opportunities. Many of us experience moments when reason abandons us and we surrender to fear or panic. If you've been hit with information that scares you or makes you highly anxious, don't join the first-down punters. Repeat the Magic Words to yourself so you can beat the fear and win the game.

46

ASK IT

The late September and early October weather had been especially warm and beautiful in New York City. During the second week of October, the temperature took a nosedive, and for the first time Leslie dressed her one-year-old son, Jake, in heavy clothes for his trip to the park. She snapped him into plaid, flannel-lined Oshkoshes, tugged him into a tiny jacket, plunked a hat on his sweet little head, and wheeled his stroller in the direction of the playground. Her park friends, mothers sitting on the benches and watching their children play, commented that the wind-chill factor would soon bring an end to their daily outings.

When she arrived home, Leslie's apartment was cold, and Jake was sniffling. She turned on the heat, but no knocking greeted her from the radiators. It'll go on soon, she said to herself. That night, Leslie and her husband Jim slept with a blanket over their down comforter. Jim had a crack-of-dawn meeting. When Leslie woke to get Jake from his crib, the apartment was still cold, and Jake's eyes were red, his nose runny. Damn it, where was the heat? She thought she remembered that there was a city ordinance requiring heat be turned on if the temperature went below 55 degrees. Surely it was even chillier than that.

The morning newspaper was waiting on her welcome mat, and as she picked it up, the neighbor across the hall was closing his front door behind him.

"Hey, Marty," Leslie greeted him. "Cold enough for you?"

Marty replied that it was so cold in his apartment, he'd sat by a blazing fire in his living room the evening before, adding, "I wonder where the heat is," as the elevator door closed on him.

When Leslie got back to her kitchen, she dialed the building's maintenance man. "Al, what's with the heat?" She was fuming. "Jake's sick and we're freezing here. So's Mr. Turnowsky. What's wrong with the furnace? Isn't there a law that says you have to turn the heat on if it's this cold?"

"Miz Ryland," the super responded. "Yeah, sure, I could turn the heat on, but no one asked me to. So I just figured everything was okay. Saves the owner money when I keep the furnace off. I'll go and do it right now."

Leslie had taken it for granted that warmth would be provided when it became cold enough. Apparently Marty and her other neighbors believed the same thing. Amazingly, not one of the sixty-eight tenants had called maintenance to ask that the heat be turned on or to inquire why it hadn't been.

We have Magic Words for all those folks: *Ask it.*

For some reason, many people seem reluctant to ask for what they need or want. We don't know why this is so, but we see it all the time. Take travel. We have an acquaintance, Jennifer, who, upon being shown any hotel room—except the presidential suite—asks if there's anything else available. She believes that managers show the inferior rooms first. So she automatically asks for something better—at the same price—and eight out of ten times she gets it. Have you ever found yourself in a room that smelled of stale cigarettes or faced a noisy main drag and not asked to see other accommodations? If so, you definitely need *ask it*.

There is one area where Ask It is absolutely and unequivocally essential. "Patients who don't ask don't get the best from their physicians," affirms a well-known cardiologist. By now, most Americans have heard via TV, newspapers, magazines, or the Internet that a well-informed patient is the best kind, and the one most likely to stay healthy. But we still know many people who are reluctant to ask doctors the kinds of questions that they want—and need—answers to.

Some people feel it's too aggressive to ask for something they need done, or to push for an answer to a question. You can't afford to be shy, especially when your welfare—or your family's—is at stake. Remember that Ask It doesn't mean you have to be overbearing or demanding. You are asking legitimate and important questions. You deserve respect—and answers.

47

STEP BACK TO GET CLOSER

We call these Magic Words our "Big Decision Words." We got them quite a few years ago from a man one of us worked for. His name was Douglas, and he was both a boss and a mentor. Douglas headed up the editorial department of a large publishing company. Along with the president of the company, he had the final say on all important books acquired by the firm. He was tall and reserved and had that rare trait in business: he was a good listener. In difficult and complicated negotiations he was always the calm eye of the storm. No matter how contentious these dealings became, Douglas, unlike many of his adversaries, never raised his voice. When things seemed to be reaching an emotional peak that threatened to derail the whole process, he would slowly get up and say, "Excuse me. I just remembered that I have to call my wife. It's a personal matter. I'll be back in a few minutes." When he returned—and it was not a few minutes, but rather more like fifteen—tempers on the other side had invariably ratcheted down, and the negotiations would resume on a smoother plane. After watching Douglas in numerous volatile situations over the years, I asked him why, at the toughest point in the deal, he would always have to step outside to place a personal call.

"Oh, that," he answered with a laugh. "I can think of only one or two times when I actually left to make a call. Once it was to my accountant to discuss something about my income tax return."

"You never called your wife?"

"Nope. If I had something I had to discuss with her, I'd do it before the meeting."

"Then what did you do?"

"Generally, I'd take a nice slow walk around the block. Sometimes I'd slip into an empty office and make myself comfortable. I was trying to step back from the tension and the fray and see the situation in a new light. Occasionally, I'd realize that the other side was right. Other times I'd see another way to reach a solution that could work for both of us."

"Does it always work?"

"There's nothing that always works, but it works enough for me to use it a lot. When I was a kid I was painfully near-sighted. Before I was fitted with the right glasses, I would look at a painting with my nose almost touching it. It's a great way to appreciate the brushwork but a lousy way to look at a painting. Later, I understood that the same principle worked for most important matters. You have to step back to get closer. Recently, when my wife and I were making a decision on buying a house, I told the real-estate agent, who was pressuring us to make an immediate offer, that we had suddenly gotten hungry—very hungry. We'd get back to her after lunch. We then had a pleasant meal where we didn't discuss the house until dessert. After a few minutes of discussion we both knew that it was the right house for us. I called the realtor while my wife was having her coffee and closed the deal.

You'll find that these Magic Words not only help you but frequently help the person on the other side. In certain tense union negotiations, they call it a "cooling-off period." In football and other sports, it's simply a "time-out." When you say "Step Back to Get Closer" to yourself, you'll always be able to see the forest *and* the trees.

48

SO, [YOUR NAME GOES HERE],

WHY ARE YOU BUYING THIS?

Deborah is in a class by herself when it comes to shopping. At one point in her life she owned a successful art gallery, so she has a terrific "eye" and her taste is impeccable and original. The stuff she buys is wonderful and has become the envy of all the "material girls" in her neighborhood. We are quite certain Deborah invented the sport of "aerobic shopping." When she's in a particularly enticing shopping locale, our gold medalist starts at opening time, sprinting in and out of as many outlet stores, warehouse sales, and exclusive boutiques as she can fit into a day. Grabbing her lunch from the takeout line at the nearest coffee shop, she stays on her feet for eight to ten hours at a stretch. She's moving so fast that she probably burns any extra calories she may accumulate eating the local delicacies.

Recently Deborah was pregnant. After the first trimester, she took off for Italy with her best friend. Morning sickness and nausea cramped her style a bit, but she came back with stunning treasures. You'd think a child would put a damper on her globe-trotting ways, but it wasn't so. When her adorable daughter, Natalie, was old enough to travel, she'd accompany her mother on trips to Paris and Hong Kong, Deb's favorite shopping spots. When Deborah was pregnant with her second child, she had to stay in town a bit more. However, eBay and other Internet shopping, the advent of 24/7 store hours, the rise of new and improved flea markets, and a rash of new emporiums kept her busy and in buoyant spirits. After her son was born, Deb quickly regained her stamina and burned off any unwanted weight within days by shopping.

Is she a compulsive shopper? Deborah doesn't think so.

"I've thought about that issue, but I only buy stuff that I need or like. I buy for friends, and I'm extravagant about presents and gift-giving at the holidays. I almost always stay within budget, and I make sure I don't owe on my credit cards. So I don't think I'm compulsive. I just really, really love to shop," she explains.

We're not qualified to make a professional diagnosis when it comes to Deborah's shopping habits, but we do have some Magic Words that we think she could use. We advise her to ask herself, *"So, Deb, why are you buying this?"*

If you're a woman—or a man—who feels a nasty tug at the pit of your stomach when you reach home after a shopping spree and tote up how much you've spent, the next time you are about to fork over cash or your credit card, pause for a full twenty seconds and ask yourself the Magic Words.

"So, [fill in your name here], why are you buying this?" Do you really need the expensive parakeet cage? How will it improve your life? Will this purchase make a difference to you next week? If that money can be better used for something else, lock up your wallet and march away from temptation.

There is, however, a caveat here. There are times when you should treat yourself in a special way. When you ask yourself the Magic Words, "Why am I buying [this digital camera, this CD, these Manolo Blahnik stilettos or lacy bras]?" and the answer is "because I really deserve a special treat," we say, the hell with it, be fabulously, superbly extravagant, indulge yourself to the max, and sashay out of the store feeling as special as you really are. As long as these occasional "treats" don't become a regular occurrence or send you to the poorhouse, you're doing just fine.

But if, after you've taken that twenty seconds to ask yourself, "Why are you buying this?" the answer is, "Jim's got one" or "It's not my size, but I just know it'll fit when I've lost some weight," turn around and head for the door—quickly.

49

MIRROR, MIRROR,
WHO THE HELL AM I?

How do you know who you really are? How can you judge if you're an honorable and decent human being? Questions like this are the most serious kind, and the most challenging, but if you're a thoughtful person, they're the questions that must be asked—and answered.

A person can be kind, loving, and generous some of the time, and mean and snarky at other times. Unless you are a saint, you probably have both good and bad traits. In our own lives, we try to make sure that the positives outweigh the negatives, and we do our best to surround ourselves with friends who do the same. Dr. John Train, a sage doctor who is now in his eighties, is a man who's seen every side of human nature. He's the one who inspired these Magic Words: *Mirror, mirror, who the hell am I?*

Every so often, stand in front of a mirror and take a good, long look at yourself. Here are some inquiries you might want to make of that person who's facing you.

Are you the kind of person you want to be?

Are you fair? Generous? Dependable?

Are you loyal?

Are you kind?

Do you really care about others?

What does love mean to you?

Can you love deeply?

Can you put another's needs before your own? Are you doing that?

What are your deepest fears? Are they real? How can you dispel them? If there is nothing that can be done, how can you live with them?

How much courage do you have?

Do you tell the truth to yourself?

Are you telling the truth now?

The "mirror test" is no pop quiz. The answers require unflinching honesty and can't be found in any book—and, most importantly, you give out your own grade.

In a world where greed and self-interest seem to be spreading every day, it's worth checking out where you stand. But watch out for instant answers—if yours come too quickly, you might be trying to pull a fast one. Step back, spray on a little Windex for the soul, and gaze deeply into the looking-glass once more. You might well see some things you wish weren't there, but serious mirror-gazing is the essential first step in getting to be the person you know you can be.

Magic Words

YOU SAY TO OTHERS

50

THIS STRESS BELONGS TO YOU

Maryanne had been a colicky baby, an infant who entered this world worried and fretful, a child who grew up serious and a bit fussy. As a young adult, Maryanne was always the dependable one, the person who took care of the details, the responsible managing editor of the university newspaper who made sure everyone met their deadlines, the designated driver, the reliable friend. During her college days she honed her wonderful, wacky sense of humor, and she was surrounded by a group of loyal pals who adored her generous heart and warm spirit and kidded her about her perpetual state of stress and distress.

When she graduated, she married a lawyer and had two children. She worried about them constantly, but she was a great mother. As they grew older and were in school all day, Maryanne decided to become a real-estate broker. The family lived in a fancy suburb where the market was skyrocketing, and there was a great deal of money waiting to be made. Maryanne aced the license test and joined the top firm in the area. It was a cutthroat place. Everyone was out to get listings, to find rich clients, to close deals. She constantly had to watch her back or another broker would steal her exclusive, or stealthily lure away her prospective buyers.

Maryanne's worrying served her well in this atmosphere. She worried about the details of all her deals, she worried about other agents trying to filch her customers, she worried about the economy, the mortgage rates, the tax hikes, she worried about every word in every contract she pored over. Despite the aura of stress and anxiety she projected, her diligence and attention to detail turned her into one of the top brokers in the region.

When Maryanne entered into a partnership with another award-winning broker, Mark, both had the highest hopes for their new venture. Mark was smart, ambitious, and resilient, and Maryanne's worrying ways did not bother him—at first. As the market tightened and deals became harder to come by, Maryanne would walk into Mark's office at least seven or eight times a day and recite a litany of her worries. Her anxieties were contagious. They started to give Mark serious heebie-jeebies and long sleepless nights.

More and more office time was spent rehashing details and fretting over the maneuvering of other brokers rather than seeking new clients and new listings. Even though Maryanne still kept Mark laughing with her sharp wit and funny observations, he found himself becoming increasingly agitated and nervous. One day, Maryanne entered Mark's office and launched into what was bothering her about a deal she was involved with.

"Maryanne," Mark responded, "it's your deal. Not mine. I don't bring all my concerns to you. We're partners in this business but *your stress belongs to you.*"

Stress is an infectious disease. When someone is suffering from it, anyone in close proximity is likely to catch it. If your mate, a friend, or a co-worker can't control anxiety, say the Magic Words as soon as you feel the stress beginning to creep toward you. If you know the person well enough, suggest ways they can deal with tension: yoga, meditation, hypnosis, or even just willpower. Stress is like the flu, except instead of hitting us seasonally, it's out there twelve months a year. If you're exposed, use Mark's Magic Words as an inoculation.

51

ARE YOU ACTUALLY
YELLING AT ME?

Most of the people we know don't yell. Maybe they did when they were kids, but they got over it. Unfortunately, quite a few other people didn't. These blunt Magic Words are to be used on the occasional yellers you might come across. Why are they blunt? Because you need Magic Words that can hammer home a message to these people.

Too many of us today are surrounded by people who fly off the handle for little or no reason. Maybe it's the times we live in, or maybe—and this is far more likely—it's just them. They get louder and louder, finally screaming at the slightest annoyance. We know one executive, Henry, who took a lot of abuse in the form of screaming sessions from his boss. One day, he finally couldn't take it anymore, and he quit. His boss had just concluded a screaming session by grabbing a paperweight off Henry's desk and throwing it at him. The object missed Henry but tore a large gash in the wall behind his desk. While Henry was clearing out his belongings, he had a carpenter come into his office and cut out the piece of wall where the paperweight had landed. Today he's the CEO of a major company—and on his desk, mounted on a piece of polished marble, is the crushed piece of plaster that was removed from his old office. It's in view at all times.

"If I ever get close to raising my voice to someone, I just look at that piece of plaster. It always works," he told us. "But with others, I find that saying, 'Are you actually yelling at me?' is like throwing a bucket of ice water in their faces. It not only gets their attention, it stops them cold."

Another friend of ours, Sheldon, a well-known executive at a large publishing house, regularly deals with arrogant agents, angry authors, and belligerent venders. Frequently, they become verbally abusive. He's found the perfect antidote in these Magic Words.

"As the decibel level starts to rise, I say, very quietly and evenly, 'Frank, are you yelling at me? Actually yelling?' And before he even has a chance to answer, I start to laugh." Sheldon swears that it works almost every time. "When that doesn't lower the decibel level, I repeat, 'You're still yelling, and I'm going to do something quite simple.' The person yelling always asks, 'What?' I just say, 'Hang up the phone right now.'"

Yellers come in all shapes and sizes, and you're likely to run into them no matter where you go. Chances are they've been yellers so long, they have no idea that there are other, easier and less stressful ways to handle things. So the next time the barking begins, keep calm and in a casual tone say, "Are You Actually Yelling at Me?" In the silence that follows, state your point and show someone just how easy it is to solve problems and get things done when you're speaking in a normal, professional, and, most importantly, respectful voice.

52

WHISKERS

Sarah had just started living with Matt, and things were going great—except for one trait of Matt's that drove Sarah crazy. Matt, who in every other respect was a pretty macho guy, became a "restaurant wimp" as soon as he stepped into any dining room that took credit cards.

For starters, Sarah was the one who always called for reservations. That didn't bother her much. What did bug her was that when they entered a restaurant, Matt would hang back, suddenly timid as a kitten, unable to step up to the maitre d' to let him know they'd arrived. People would show up after them and be seated earlier. Matt was also content to be seated anywhere as long as there was a roof over his head. Whether it was noisy, positioned inches from the kitchen, or in the path of a freezing draft, any table was fine with him. If the service was atrocious and the waiters were gabbing in the corner, he made no effort to get their attention.

She decided to discuss the problem with Matt. Yes, he said, she was right. He would shape up. But he quickly slipped back in to his old passive ways, which irritated—no, angered was the more accurate word—Sarah no end.

She started thinking about exactly what it was that bothered her. She was a "modern woman," after all, and it certainly wouldn't hurt her to tell the maitre d' where she'd like to sit. But, even though it was a bit old-fashioned, she still enjoyed being "taken care of"—at least in restaurant situations. It really wasn't that big a deal that Matt didn't take charge when they had dinner out, but it would make their evenings seem more romantic if he did. Finally she came up with a great idea to solve the problem. "When you start hanging back," she said, "I'll just remind you by saying one word, like 'gentleman,' or 'gumption.' No one else will know what I'm talking about, and only you will understand." Matt liked the concept but felt that both words were too obvious. He thought someone might wise up to their trick, and he'd be embarrassed. He pondered for a few minutes and suggested the word "whiskers," which immediately signaled "be a man" to him.

A few days later Matt and Sarah had just been served some champagne at a crowded party celebrating the publication of a friend's book. They were talking to a vivacious octogenarian they'd just met.

"That champagne looks refreshing," the woman said.

"Why don't you take mine?" Sarah offered her glass.

They continued to talk for a moment or two. Sarah didn't want to leave the woman alone, but she wanted another drink, so when she was sure she wouldn't be seen by their companion, she mouthed the word "whiskers." Matt got the hint right away and said, "Please excuse me for a moment, ladies. I'm going to find some champagne for Sarah. I'll be right back."

Sarah was delighted that the Magic Word worked, and Matt was happy that Sarah was happy. "Whiskers" was such a success that they invented other magic words to get through sticky situations. Matt often thought that Sarah was driving too close to the car in front of them. She strongly disagreed with him, and they would get into a nasty argument about it. But they both hated quarrelling and knew how corrosive it could be, so they cooked up a word to solve the highway problem: if you drive too close, you'll thump the bumper, thus their Magic Word "thumpers" was invented to cool tempers and prevent accidents. Sarah told us they used their Magic Words very sparingly and only when absolutely necessary—if used too much, they lose their power.

"Whiskers," of course, had meaning only for Matt and Sarah. As writing partners, here are some words we use all the time, "decibella," "six seven nine," "ice tray," and "side chair." Since they're our own personal words, we're not telling you what they mean. The fun of "Whiskers" is discovering expressions that are significant only for you and for the situation you find yourself in.

53

I'VE DECIDED NOT TO DECIDE

In the eleventh year of his marriage to Lauren, Gary developed a roving eye. On business trips, Gary would sit alone at the hotel bar, nursing a glass of wine and hoping that an attractive woman would sit next to him. In his fantasies, the woman would come on to him, and he would be powerless to keep from following her to her room where. . . . At this point he would will himself to think of Lauren and his vows to her.

Finally, it happened. Gary cheated on his wife, and it made him miserable. Torn between lying or devastating Lauren, he decided to do neither. Instead he went to a therapist and after several sessions realized that there was one major problem in his marriage (as well as some significant smaller ones). Lauren, whom he'd met in grad school, was five years older than he was, and, at the time they married, they had both agreed that they didn't want children. Now Gary had changed his mind.

Lauren's biological clock had run out, and unless they adopted, children were an impossibility. Lauren was adamant about not adopting. Either Gary stayed in the marriage, gave up his desire for children, and resolved there would be no more cheating, or he owed it to himself, and to Lauren, to leave. His therapist recommended couples' therapy but told Gary straightforwardly he believed that, underneath it all, Gary really wanted out of the marriage.

Reluctant to make a decision, Gary urged Lauren to join him in therapy. The sessions improved their communication, but they didn't stop him from having a one-nighter with a woman named Jean. It bloomed into a passionate affair. Jean could have children, and he thought she would make a wonderful wife and mother. He believed he was deeply in love with her, but he also felt he was still in love with Lauren. As the affair progressed, Jean gave him an ultimatum: "Get out of the marriage, or it's over."

"Give me a month," he responded. "It takes time to break up a decade-long relationship, and I don't want to hurt Lauren. I'll be with you in a month."

Eight weeks went by, and still Gary had not left Lauren, who suspected that Gary was playing around but had decided to ignore his more frequent "business trips." Jean repeated her ultimatum, but this time she gave him two more months.

Gary was in agony. He loved Jean, he felt deeply for Lauren. How could he decide between them? Again, he saw the therapist, who chipped away at the reasons for his indecision. Finally, he counseled Gary to make up his mind. Life was short, he wanted children, what was stopping him? But Gary simply could not decide.

He quit therapy, and spent a long weekend alone on a remote island. He promised himself he would make his decision by the end of the weekend. On Sunday night he was no nearer to a resolution than he had been on Friday or in the year and a half since he'd met Jean. Coming back on the plane, he had an insight that gave him some of the relief he desperately needed.

"I will decide not to decide," he told himself. "I have finally made a decision. And it is to make no decision at this point. It is simply impossible for me to make a choice. I'm not ready. So I've decided not to decide."

Gary's problem was an extreme version of what many of us feel as we face turning points in life. Gary was indecisive because he was ambivalent. When you're ambivalent, you believe one hundred percent in each of two contradictory things. It's an excruciating feeling and can also result in real hurt to other people in your life. Gary strongly believed his marriage would survive, and he believed with equal intensity that he should get a divorce. Therapy had helped him see the deep fissures in his marriage and given him some knowledge about himself, but the therapist couldn't make his decision for him. At that point in his life, he simply wasn't ready to divorce. He could only decide which road to take when his interior clock struck the right hour, in other words, when he resolved his ambivalence. Gary knew it wasn't a great position for him to be in, but it wasn't as bad as making a decision that might be wrong. Lauren soon found out about the other woman and left Gary, but he still feels that his decision not to decide was the only one he could make under the extreme emotional duress he felt. His and Lauren's separation and divorce resolved his ambivalence, and he began to get on with his life.

Many times we face decisions we're unprepared—or unable—to make. Saying the Magic Words to yourself—"I've Decided Not to Decide"—can alleviate the intense pressure of making a choice until you can climb out of the ambivalence hole. Make sure you're not just putting off a difficult decision—if you're genuinely ambivalent, these words can really help.

54

LET'S QUIT WHILE WE'RE BEHIND

No one will dispute that it makes sense to quit while you're ahead. But there are times in life when you're behind, and you've got to cut your losses and walk away. Don't forget that many battles throughout history have been won by strategic retreats. Knowing how to back off at the proper moment is always helpful, and sometimes vital.

Gary, a commodities trader from Chicago, was about to make his first visit to the parents of his girlfriend, and soon-to-be fiancée, Ursula. She had told Gary a number of times that her father was a rabid Chicago White Sox fan. Gary, who doesn't follow sports very closely, decided to bone up on the White Sox to try to make a good impression. After two weeks of reading up on the team and talking to a number of friends who followed the Sox closely, he felt ready to talk to his prospective father-in-law.

Before dinner at Ursula's parents' house, while she and her mother were in the kitchen preparing the meal, Gary sat down for a drink with William, Ursula's father. At first they made small talk about where Gary had gone to school, then shifted to the election that was coming up in a few months. They were in agreement on the candidates, so that conversation didn't last very long. Gary then saw his opportunity to talk about the White Sox. He told William he had been a fan of theirs since grade school and then went on to comment about the team's performance that year. William listened intently and then asked Gary a few questions about the Sox bullpen. Gary scrambled for an answer, trying to be both knowledgeable and vague. Then William asked him about one of the great White Sox players, Minnie Minoso. The name was, in fact, familiar to him (who could forget a name that distinctive?), but that was the limit of Gary's knowledge about the player. He looked at Ursula's father for a long moment before saying, "You know what. I'm going to quit while I'm behind. I've been a Sox fan for about two whole weeks now." William reached for the wine and filled Gary's glass.

"You know, Gary, that's the nicest compliment I think I've ever had."

"I'm not following you, sir," he said.

"Well, I could tell almost immediately that you didn't know a thing about the White Sox, and I was mystified as to why you were trying to convince me that you did. But the fact that you tried to learn something about them in order to talk to me is very flattering. I think you and I have a chance at being friends."

Gary reached out and shook Ursula's father's hand. "I want to thank you, sir."

"Thank me for what?" asked William.

"For being a fan of baseball instead of ballet. You see, I know absolutely nothing about ballet, and with a ballet company, it would have taken me months just to get where I am now on the White Sox."

The next time you find yourself in a situation like Gary's, just say, "I'm Going to Quit While I'm Behind," and then gracefully fold your hand. This type of awkward situation can easily escalate until you've gone from being merely silly to seeming dumb. Don't dig yourself a deep hole unless you're planting a tree.

55

We know a man who's perfected the art of reading upside down. Memos, notes, budgets, bills, letters—nothing escapes his wrong-way reading. He's so deft, you'd never suspect what he's up to, but he's taking in everything that you might want to keep private. We've learned to clear our desks and close our drawers when he's in sight. This guy's not unique. There are quite a few people sniffing around who are way too inquisitive. All of us have some personal classified information, stuff that we don't want others to know about. Sometimes you'll encounter brazen snoopers, women and men who probe for data you don't want to disclose. Other times you'll come across people whose nosiness is so subtle that at first you won't recognize what's happening. When you find yourself being given the third degree, we have a magic answer to stop nosy folks cold. These words will put an end to the following queries, which are really the equivalent of walking into someone's house without knocking on the door.

How much did you pay for your house?

Is your child on Ritalin?

Do you color your hair?

How much do you make?

What do you pay your cleaning lady?

Were you invited to so-and-so's party?

Are you taking Prozac?

Are your parents leaving you money?

Have you tried Viagra?

When did you have a facelift/nose job/lipo?

How much are you worth?

That's just a sampling of the kinds of questions audacious people will ask. We were at a cocktail party where a young woman was being circled by a snooper. They were discussing real-estate prices, and the snooper wanted to know how much the woman had paid for a piece of property she'd recently bought. The woman looked her inquisitor straight in the eye.

"Why are you asking?" she said.

The snooper was stopped cold. For a moment, he was literally speechless. He quickly retreated by saying he needed to freshen his drink and wandering off toward the bar. Our heroine's comeback was so drop-dead effective that it immediately made our top-ten list of magic words. So next time you're being bullied into disclosing private information, don't beat around the bush or let yourself get flustered. Square your shoulders, look the questioner right in the eye, and ask your own tough question: "Why Are You Asking?"

56

HOW ABOUT LETTING ME BE A
PILLOW OF STRENGTH?

Steffie was going through a very rough patch. Her husband, Andrew, who was seventeen years older than her, had been cheating on Steffie with a woman who was even younger than she was. Andrew wanted to marry this other woman and demanded a divorce. Steffie had quit law school to marry Andrew, and when she had her son, Will, she decided to become a full-time mother. Her degree could wait, she told herself. Raising a child was the most important thing to her. Andrew was an angry and tightfisted man. Even though he was the one suing for divorce—and a very successful lawyer himself—he didn't want Steffie to have any child support. Plus he told her she had to get out of their house, which was in his name. On top of her emotional pain, she was now panicked about money. How would she make a living? How could she survive with no career and no prospects? Who would take care of Will?

Judy was Steffie's devoted best friend. She saw Steffie at least a few times a week, and spoke to her on the phone once or twice a day. She drove Will to play dates and took Steffie shopping because Andrew had simply driven off with their car. Except for Judy (and Will, of course) Steffie felt alone in the world—she'd been so shocked and heartbroken over her situation that she hadn't even found a lawyer. She was certain that somehow she and Andrew would get back together. Judy told her to get rid of the horrible creep as fast as possible.

Then Steffie found out that Andrew's girlfriend was pregnant. She thought she'd been in pain before, but now the hurt became almost unbearable. Judy was truly concerned and got Steffie to see a pastoral counselor, driving her to and from the appointments and making sure Will was taken care of.

About this time, Judy was diagnosed with breast cancer. A day after getting this terrible news, Steffie received papers from Andrew's lawyer: he was suing Steffie for custody of Will. She had finally retained a lawyer, but Andrew's latest move put Steffie over the top.

Her first concern was Will, but Judy was almost as important. Judy was her best friend and needed her badly. Luckily the cancer hadn't spread, and Judy wouldn't need a mastectomy. Steffie decided that no matter what it cost, she needed to help Judy the way Judy had helped her. She rented a car and started driving Judy to her grueling chemo sessions. She cooked casseroles three or four times a week and brought Judy books and chocolate truffles.

Both friends were in tough situations. One night while they were talking things over on the phone, Judy said to Steffie, "I know exactly what you're going through and how much you're hurting. On top of the divorce and all that's happening, you've been a pillar of strength for me. But you can't go on like this. Nobody can carry a double burden. It's just too much. Why don't you just be a *pillow* of strength for me?"

Steffie protested that Judy was in direr straits than she was.

"Let's not try one-downs-manship," Judy said, and they both laughed.

"Okay, I'll be your pillow if you'll be my comforter," Steffie finally agreed.

Both of us believe in unconditional friendship, but there are times when you can't give your all to a friend who's facing the darkest days. If you martyr yourself in the name of friendship, you'll only end up resenting your friend. Yet you want to be able to promise a friend that you'll do everything you can do to help. That's when "How About Letting Me Be a Pillow of Strength?" works its magic. It lets the other person know how much you love them, and that you love yourself, too.

57

THIS IS A PEWTER OPPORTUNITY

Eleven years earlier Tony had been offered an extraordinary opportunity. He was named president of a large media company headquartered in Los Angeles—the opportunity was golden, the perks were platinum: a mansion in Beverly Hills, a stunning pied-à-terre in New York, an astronomic salary, huge bonuses, and a limitless expense account. For seven years he lived like a baron and guided the company through a strong economy. When the market began to move into a downswing, the business started to teeter, and the board voted Tony out of a job.

For a couple of years, Tony enjoyed the high life his golden parachute provided: he bought an ancient farmhouse in Tuscany and a co-op in Aspen and rented a ritzy apartment in New York. He tried his hand at writing screenplays and locating scripts to develop and produce, spending freely as he went along. One fall morning Tony woke up and realized the money was running out and admitted to himself that he was bored and dispirited. Suddenly it didn't seem like so much fun to be living in four places at once, not to mention the cash that these habitats were devouring monthly. He put out the word to friends and acquaintances that he might be in the market for a job if he could "do something interesting." He had a few of-fers, but nothing seemed right. He was looking for a major challenge, a high-profile position, and top-of-the-line bucks.

Another year flew by. He sold the farmhouse, rented out the co-op in Aspen, and let go of the apartment in New York. He took on a consulting job, for a high fee, but only for sev-eral months. Then the stock market went south, and his port-folio diminished alarmingly—he had to find something or else he'd be living on a very, very modest budget, something he had never done before. The prospects were grim on all fronts un-til Tony went to a dinner party that a friend was giving.

He was seated next to a woman who ran a medium-sized publishing company that was expanding its Los Angeles base. She knew Tony's name from the media world, and after they got to talking she asked if he'd be interested in working with her. They met for lunch the next day, and she outlined what she had in mind. Tony would be a senior vice president in charge of overseeing two new properties the company had re-cently acquired. He would be headquartered in a small office in L.A., and the pay would be about a quarter of what he'd been making in his heyday. He'd share a secretary with two other people, and his bonus—potentially a very generous one—would be based on performance. Tony said he'd mull it over.

During the next two days Tony did some hard thinking and talked to several friends about the offer. This job was a comedown for him, a big one. On the other hand, it presented an interesting and possibly very lucrative challenge. But he was mighty unhappy about the salary, the dingy offices, the lack of an expense account, and he confessed to his best friend Jonathan that he felt his professional pride was at stake.

Jonathan, a successful doctor and a very thoughtful guy, had seen Tony through the last decade's ups and downs. He reminded Tony of the isolation and despair he felt at not having an office to go to or a challenge to sink his teeth into—or a check to cash every month.

"You can take an early retirement and live on your pension in a humble way or you can take this job," he told Tony, "Most people never get the kind of golden opportunity you were given years ago. You were incredibly lucky. You had a great run. But *this is a pewter opportunity*. It's a very nice deal. You'd be crazy to pass it up."

As Tony reflected on what his friend said, he thought about pewter. Pewter was nothing to be embarrassed about—it might not be as precious or shiny as gold, but pewter is a valued and beautiful metal that's been used by the finest craftsmen for centuries. It's strong, and with the right attention, it, too, can gleam. Jonathan was absolutely right, Tony realized. Pewter opportunities don't sparkle that much, and it's possible to overlook one. Whenever you are offered an opportunity but it's not exactly what you had in mind, take time to assess the situation and see what's really in it for you. If you're aware of pewter opportunities, you'll be surprised at how often they come your way.

58

LET'S READ THE
WRITING ON THE WALL

Have you ever noticed that when you have an argument with a friend, a colleague, or a partner, it's usually over an issue that you've argued about in the past?

Dan is a packrat. Sue is a minimalist. She wants every surface bare and sparkling clean. Dan loves a cluttered desk and an occasional speck of dust. They clash all the time over their housekeeping styles.

Jeff's and Henry's politics put them on opposite sides of every subject. Even though they are good golf buddies, they seem to forget that they inhabit two different planets where their worldviews are concerned, and they always end up irritated or angry when they try to discuss current events.

Melinda and her mother have always disagreed about clothes. Melinda thinks her mother is beautiful but dresses in a dowdy way; her mom feels Melinda's miniskirts and tank tops are too provocative. Their arguments have been going on for twenty years.

Olivia and Charlie both work for a well-known recruiting firm. When a company hires them to find candidates for a job, Olivia often presents people who have out-of-the-ordinary qualifications but don't really fit the job description. Charlie can't believe Olivia doesn't follow the tried-and-true recruiting rules. His candidates must fit the mold or they aren't presented to clients. Both Charlie's and Olivia's contenders land top jobs regularly. At weekly meetings, when the staff discusses new recruiting projects, the two of them invariably lock horns, much to the discomfort of their co-workers.

Years ago, in an area that had been decimated by riots, Howard came across a telling piece of graffiti scrawled across the crumbling brick wall of a burned-out building: *Read the writing on the wall.* It was a chilling reminder that some situations are set to explode, and it doesn't take much to light the fuse. Experience with friends, family, and co-workers should teach us that some subjects are potentially dangerous and will never be resolved. Instead of wearing ourselves down with futile fighting, both of us now envision that ruined wall, and, when explosives are present, saying the Magic Words to ourselves keeps us from lighting a match. When you're dealing with someone you inevitably fight or argue with, try explaining the Magic Words to them. It can keep both of you safely away from the minefield.

59

LET ME THINK ABOUT IT

Meredith has been a friend of ours for a long time. She is a very smart, very lovable gal, but, like a lot of people we know, she's also very impatient. She likes things to be done at two speeds—fast and faster. She gets antsy if she has to wait for a check at the restaurant or stand in line for a ticket. She's also impulsive. Jumps to conclusions. Makes snap decisions. She bought an SUV in five minutes. Decided, in a heartbeat, to scrap a slow-moving project at the office. Bid on a trip to Albany at a charity auction—and won.

Most of Merri's decisions are sound, but some she regrets—she really wasn't interested in spending a long weekend in the capital of New York State. After scrapping the office project, she realized it might have brought her important new sources of income if she'd given it a bit more time.

When Merri was promoted to a top executive position, her company suggested she work with a consultant to help her develop a more prudent management style. She welcomed the opportunity. We had lunch with Merri a few weeks after her promotion to see how things were working out with the new job. The consultant, it turned out, had worked with her for just two days.

"Did you fire him?" we asked.

"Not at all. He told me I didn't need him anymore."

"What did he do?"

Within the first few hours of meeting Merri, the expert had sized her up and given her a small white card with five words hand-printed on it: *Let me think about it.*

He suggested that she slip the card into her jacket pocket and hold on to it when she felt a knee-jerk reaction coming on. Not that her impulses were bad. Mostly they were on target, but when they weren't, it could cost her dearly in her new position. Plus it was important for Merri's staff to know that their boss took the time to think through a situation and make thoughtful, careful decisions.

The words "Let me think about it" are some of the most useful and usable Magic Words in this book. Try them in a doctor's office when he suggests an expensive test, say them when you're asked for your opinion on a tricky or crucial issue, avail yourself of them when you need to stall for time. There are dozens of ways those six syllables can make your life easier and more rewarding

60

PLEASE, DON'T BE SO RUDE

Today rudeness flourishes from coast to coast. Sales clerks, wait-ers, nurses, plumbers, doctors—many of those who serve the public could, in our opinion, profit from a lesson in manners. Take the travel industry, for example. Those who fly the skies often find they're not as friendly as they're supposed to be. Air-ports are so clogged, and the airways so crowded, that it comes as no surprise when tempers flare and rudeness erupts.

Our friend Tom was taking off for a well-deserved vaca-tion in the Caribbean. At the crack of dawn, as he threaded his way to the counter through people, luggage, surfboards, and animal crates, he felt his blood pressure rising. Long lines with cranky children snaked toward the check-in counter. The take-off was delayed, so he stood for ten very long minutes in a queue at the understaffed coffee counter waiting for a luke-warm latté.

Finally, boarding began. A stewardess took his boarding pass, waved him onboard with a big smile, and wished him a pleasant trip. Buoyed by her pleasant send-off, he coiled his legs into the cramped space and immediately reached for a book to bury himself in until refreshments were offered. Even though he rarely drank, he planned on ordering himself some champagne, mixing it with orange juice, and snoozing peacefully all the way down to Barbados. After all, it was the beginning of his vacation, and Tom intended to enjoy it to the max.

After a few minutes his legs started to go numb. He checked out the overhead compartments for pillows and blankets so he could use them to maneuver himself into a more comfortable position, but all he could see was crammed luggage. He tried to flag down a flight attendant for a pillow, but no one paid any attention. Even though the temperature outside was 24 degrees, the air-conditioning started to whirr, and frigid drafts swirled around the passengers' heads. People around him were coughing and sneezing. He tried once more to get the attention of a flight attendant, this time to inquire if the temperature could be moderated. As he looked up and down the aisle, he spotted one nonchalantly filing her nails by the galley and talking nonstop to her two co-workers. No one seemed to notice the passengers' obvious discomfort.

Finally, Tom twisted himself out of his seat and headed toward the group. He stood next to the threesome and waited to be recognized. Finally, he interrupted their conversation.

"Would it be possible to lower the air-conditioning?" he asked frostily.

"Close the nozzle over your seat," one attendant replied curtly.

"Could I possibly have a blanket then?" Tom asked icily.

"They're in the overhead compartments," said another.

Tom was so infuriated that he had a momentary urge to knock their heads together. Instead he gave them a big smile and beseeched them, "Please, don't be so rude."

The group suddenly turned to face him. He repeated his

words and grinned charmingly from ear to ear even though he felt like throttling them.

Momentarily flummoxed by Tom's big smile and his plea, the flight attendants snapped to attention as their humanity returned. "I'm sorry, sir," one of them responded, "what can I get you? Let me talk to the captain about the cabin air, and I'm sure I can locate some pillows for you."

Most of us recognize that life is more complicated and more rushed than ever before. The majority of flight attendants conduct themselves professionally, and many go far beyond the call of duty in doing their jobs. Ditto for sales clerks, taxi drivers, plumbers, landscapers, lawyers, nurses, and phone operators. But some people are just plain insolent and impertinent. And still more get used to being rude automatically, even when they don't mean to. (Admit it. You've probably done this yourself.) We're aware that their bad attitude could be caused by a million things: a lover's quarrel, anxiety about the next mortgage payment, a sick child, the stresses of just living from one day to the next. When you come across unpleasant behavior from someone who should know better, use the Magic Words— and make sure to use them with your biggest toothpaste-ad smile.

61

A STIFF UPPER LIP SHOULD
TREMBLE NOW AND THEN

"Your mother lives with your family?" we asked Doreen, a woman who had just moved into Howard's neighborhood. We'd been discussing the complicated situations that arose from having aging parents.

"Every day with her is a gift," Doreen told us. "She's been with us for almost two years. Ted adores her and the kids can't leave her alone. They're always wanting her to play with them."

When we met her mother, the famous Jule, we enjoyed her company enormously and immediately made a new friend. About a year after Doreen moved to the neighborhood, Jule was diagnosed with a serious heart problem. She was restricted to a wheelchair and hospitalized several times. It was a strain on the family, but Doreen never complained about the stress in her life.

Then Ted was injured in a car accident. His legs were smashed, and he would need at least a year of physical therapy before he could walk again. The constant worry was beginning to wear Doreen down. She'd been brought up by Jule to look on the bright side of things and, above all, to be utterly brave and utterly dependable in every kind of circumstance—including a household meltdown, which was what she faced daily. She hired a companion to help Ted and Jule, but money was tight and nothing was coming in. So on top of the daily stress, she was feeling enormous financial pressure.

One morning Howard and Doreen were buying groceries at the local IGA and decided to take a few minutes for a cup of coffee at the café down the street.

"I know things are really tough," Howard said. "I don't know how you manage it all."

"It's the way I was brought up. You don't complain. You don't weep. You just carry on," she said, but Howard could see she was near tears.

"Listen, what you're going through is more than a person should be expected to bear," he said. "Just remember, *a stiff upper lip should tremble now and then* when things are tough.

A tear escaped from the corner of her eye. She pretended not to notice and finished her coffee. Howard was signaling for the check when Doreen said quietly, "I was never allowed to do that."

"Think about it," said Howard. "Not even professional boxers can take a daily pounding. Right now you may find it hard to believe, but there are lots of laughs inside you, waiting to come out. They're kind of buried right now. Believe me, they'll come out someday soon. You'll laugh and you'll make others laugh. I'm not saying you'll have a career as a standup, but there are sunnier and funnier days ahead."

A couple of days later, Howard received an e-mail from Doreen thanking him for his concern and his advice. "Just hearing you talk about my situation made me feel better than I have in months. I take time off every day to let the lip tremble," she wrote, "and thanks, Howard, it really helps."

Who likes crybabies or whiners? No one. But who doesn't

understand when a person who's carrying a backbreaking load lets out a yell? Doreen never even whimpered and, as a result, unknowingly added to her burden. By trying to bury her own pain, she was causing herself real emotional damage. The next time you see someone who's handling more than one person can possibly manage, remind them how important it is to let go once in a while. And if you're the one who has the stiff upper lip, let these Magic Words be your mantra. Like a lucky stone, take them out and say them whenever you need them. They get better the more you use them.

62

I WANT TO GIVE YOU
ANOTHER SHOT

"The minute I found out for sure that Stuart was cheating on me I wasn't able to breathe. The physical pain was so intense that I got into bed and curled up like a baby. I couldn't even cry . . ."

Molly and Stuart had been married for almost five years when she discovered that her husband had been unfaithful. Here's what happened:

"Stuart works as a regional sales manager and travels to the different offices he supervises a couple of times a month. He usually spends three or four nights a week away from home. I had noticed that we'd been getting quite a few phone calls and hangups when we were home together in the evening. I'd read in some women's magazines this can be a tip-off to trouble. I'd dial *69, but the number would always be unavailable. Eventually the calls stopped and I forgot about them.

"Everything seemed really fine with Stuart and me, and then two things happened that changed my whole world. I do the bills, and there are always a few of Stu's business calls on our phone bill, so I pay no attention to them. This particular bill had several calls to a number in Chicago. For some reason I called the number, and it belonged to a hotel there. I didn't think anything about it at the time, since I recognized the name as a place that Stu stayed.

"Stu has a corporate Visa card that he uses when he travels, and I never open the bill. By mistake I opened it the same week that I called the Chicago number. There was a charge for three hundred dollars at Saks Fifth Avenue. I had a bad feeling about this. When I thought about it, I decided to call Visa and see if I could find out what the charge was for. It was a black cashmere sweater from the women's department. I started to feel sick to my stomach as soon as I hung up the phone. Then something clicked. Why had Stu been calling the hotel in Chicago? The travel office at his company did all the booking for him. I was so wildly upset that I wasn't thinking straight, but something made me call the hotel and say I was the bookkeeper for Stu's office and I wanted to check the bills. Turned out that Stuart had registered at the hotel as "Mr. and Mrs."

"I called him at the office and told him to come home. He knew from the tone of my voice that something terrible had happened, but I wouldn't tell him what it was. I confronted him with the facts. And he denied everything. Everything. Finally, I wouldn't speak to him. I just got into bed and didn't think I'd ever get out. He sat in the kitchen. About twenty minutes later, he came into the bedroom and told me he'd been with this woman he knew from the office two or three times, and it meant nothing to him. He started to cry and said it would never happen again.

"Hearing it from him only made it worse. I told him to leave. But he kept sitting on the bed and crying, telling me he'd made a terrible mistake and that he loved me with all his heart.

" 'Maybe, just maybe, I could get over a one-night stand,' I told him, and my voice was shaking so much I could hardly spit the words out, 'but you were with her more than once or twice.'

"He stayed at home the rest of the day. I couldn't leave my bed. I finally was able to cry, and then I got angry. How do you deal with betrayal? How can you ever trust a person who's done the worst thing you can think of to hurt you?"

"Finally, we agreed we should see a couples counselor. Stuart found one and called, but couldn't get an appointment for two days. Those forty-eight hours were the worst kind of nightmare. I wouldn't speak to him. I made him sleep in the living room. I told him he was dirt. Then I screamed at him and called him every rotten thing I could think of. Then I told him I wanted a divorce.

"We finally saw the therapist. I didn't think she could help much, but I had agreed to see her and I kept my word. We went over all that had happened, and then she looked at me and asked, 'Molly, can you say this? "I want to give you another shot." Unless you can tell him that and really mean it, you can't salvage the relationship.'

"I took a long time before I answered. 'I'm not sure if I can.'

"She advised us to go home, think about it, and come back on Friday. For the next two days Stuart was very quiet, and I was doing a lot of very serious thinking. He wanted to know what my decision was, but I was still suffering so much I didn't want to say anything. Finally the time came to see her. When she asked what was happening, I said, 'I want to give you another shot, Stu. It will take a lot of time for me to trust you again and I'm still angry and hurt, but let's make it work.'

"It took about a year before things were really the same as before. If that therapist hadn't said those words, I would never have been able to see the situation clearly, and we wouldn't still be married, with an adorable two-year-old and another on the way."

Sadly, we've heard many stories like this one. Relationships are built on love and respect and trust. When that trust is broken, the damage is very deep, and sometimes irreparable. But wait for the initial anguish to subside enough so that you can see the situation more clearly. The first thing you need to ask yourself is if you really want to stay in the relationship. This requires the deepest kind of reflection. Too often people are in such pain and so angry that they're willing to toss out years of love and shared experience because their partner has been unfaithful. If you consider the pros and cons of your relationship and come out believing there's real hope of reestablishing trust between the two of you, then try the Magic Words "I Want to Give You Another Shot." But you must mean what you say. You've got to give it a shot with all you've got—no halfway, halfhearted efforts. The magic lies in the sincerity. Anything else won't work.

63

LET'S HAVE A BAD TIME

In 1996, there were twenty-two snowstorms in New York, and the thermometer had broken all-time lows in the Midwest. Sam and Mandy had been very close friends for years, and they both *despised* the cold. Sam had recently relocated to Chicago from New York City, and the unrelenting wind and snow were more than he could take. Back east, Mandy was in despair over the dirty slush and never-ending bad weather. One night, as they discussed the latest storm reports on the phone, Sam said, "I maneuvered a business meeting in Los Angeles next week. I can take a few days off—why don't you meet me out there, and we can have some fun in the sun. We'll head to Disneyland, check out the surf, have real Mexican food."

Mandy switched her schedule around and met Sam in L.A. Before you could say "platonic relationship," all those years of staid friendship were out the window, and love was in the driver's seat. They spent their entire holiday at the Beachcomber, a charming oceanside hideaway that Sam had heard about. The two occasionally ventured out of their room for a bit of sun and a few margaritas—but not very often.

Then they both had to return to the real world, Sam to Chicago and Mandy to her law firm in New York. As they kissed good-bye at the airport terminal, they promised to meet again as soon as possible for a long weekend. They didn't want their newly discovered bliss to end. Sam told Mandy he'd find another place as perfect as the Beachcomber and they'd be together soon.

One night later that week, Sam called Mandy. "I haven't found the right place yet. If it's not right, I'm afraid we might have a bad time." Sam had always been a perfectionist, fearing to fall below the standards he set for himself.

"Sam," Mandy said, "what rule says that we must have a good time? Why do most people think they always have to have a good time? Let's have a bad time! The two of us will be together, and we'll face whatever happens. Together. That doesn't seem so bad to me."

Alexandra adopted Mandy's philosophy when she and Dennis took a vacation in the Caribbean with two other couples and their children. Everyone was excited about the trip, but the bad news started at the airport. Their flight was delayed by several hours, some of the baggage was lost, and when they reached the villa they'd rented, it was locked and no one was there to let them in. Finally, they settled in. The next three days brought downpours. Tempers were getting short from being cooped up for so long—and having spent so much money on the accommodations. One overcast morning as they sat quite glumly over breakfast, Alexandra announced, "Okay, we're all going to have a bad time! What's the baddest time we can have?" The younger members of the group took up the challenge and started tossing out all sorts of "bad times"—from windsurfing in a hurricane to barbecuing "mad cow" meat. Everyone joined in and started to laugh. In spite of a bad start to the morning, the Magic Words turned the day into one of fun and high spirits.

Just as Mandy had used the words to assure Sam that they didn't have to repeat their perfect first vacation, Alexandra broke the tension on *her* flawed vacation by throwing in the Magic Words. She dropped the phrase when the outlook seemed pretty bleak and turned the mood around. When you're anticipating a special event, or looking forward to any day that's supposed to be pure bliss, and you get the opposite, these Magic Words can spin the situation 180 degrees. Say them with an upbeat tone, add some energy, and a hint of sarcasm to your voice—"Let's Have a BA-A-D Time!"—and you'll see how well they work.

64

I'M MYSTIFIED

Lynn knew for a fact that the invitations to the Harrisons' gala holiday party had been mailed. She'd noticed the stylishly engraved cream-colored card on Harriet's desk at least ten days ago. So now she could safely assume that she and Herb had been dropped from the Harrisons' list.

Lynn genuinely liked both Stella and Trent Harrison and thought of them as friends. And there was no denying it. They were also major clients. As sales manager of a well-known magazine, Lynn depended on their goodwill and their pages of advertising. So why had she not been invited to their annual party, which she'd attended year after year? Could the invitation have been lost in the mail? No, they were always hand-delivered to the guest's home, a gesture that summed up the Harrisons' cultivated elegance when it came to entertaining. Had she unknowingly done something to offend them? She searched her memory but could find absolutely no cause for any bad feelings.

Of course it was only a party. Nothing more. But Lynn was genuinely hurt and upset that she'd been left out. And going would have been good for business. She called her best pal, Paige, to discuss the situation.

"If you consider them friends," Paige advised, "you ought to talk to them. There must be some mistake."

"I consider them very close, I even invited them to our tenth anniversary party," Lynn said. "But what can I say? It's humiliating to call and ask, 'Hey, why weren't we invited?' "

Lynn and Paige reached no conclusion, but Lynn mulled over the circumstances for several days. Even though she told herself it was just a silly party, she was troubled by the situation and wanted to resolve it once and for all. She looked for words that would express her feelings, words that didn't make her sound like an outsider begging to be invited. When she finally found the words she needed, she dialed Stella Harrison's number. They exchanged pleasantries, then Lynn took a deep breath and said, "Stella, I feel you're a good friend, and I just had to say that *I'm mystified* as to why we weren't invited to your party."

There was a long pause and some shuffling of papers. "But, Lynn," Stella responded, "I have my response list in front of me, your RSVP said 'No.' I was surprised and sorry that you couldn't make it, since I didn't think you two were going to be out of town." They spent a few minutes trying to untangle the mix-up—someone must have mistakenly marked a negative RSVP by Lynn's name before her invitation could be sent—and by the end of the call, the tension was eased. Lynn and Herb went to the party and had a fabulous time.

The second we heard the words, *I'm mystified*, we recognized they have a great many uses. When said in the right tone—not with anger or irritation but with perplexity—they can smooth out almost any situation that is potentially uncomfortable.

65

EVEN A FRISBEE TAKES SIDES

We like our eggs over easy. We order our vodka chilled and straight up with a twist. We prefer Hitchcock to Bergman. We order our steak medium rare, never just medium. One of us is an atheist, the other is still trying to figure it out. We're angry with some politicians, amused by others. In other words, we have likes and dislikes and, most important, opinions. Generally, strong ones. We care about things, and we take sides. Indifference really bugs us. We frequently run across people who are proud of what we call their "superior indifference," like a man we encountered at a party we recently attended who, in the course of conversation, was asked,

"What do you think of Stalin?"

"A terrible guy, of course, but you have to remember he kept the ethnic antagonisms of the different Soviet states in check. There was no war in Chechnya during the Stalin years."

"Yes, but at a cost of forty million lives."

Pol Pot, gun control, Genghis Khan, nuclear power, the Manson family, abortion rights, you name it, this person, clothed in "superior indifference," would probably be incapable of coming down definitively on either side of an issue. Is this any way to live life? Life, for better or worse, is about taking sides.

"When I first met Hank," Abbey told us, "I liked him immediately. He was smart, generous, and funny. The thing about him that maddened me was that he shied away from having a strong opinion about anything that was even mildly controversial. He was a registered Democrat but wouldn't criticize Republican positions. He was against capital punishment but could see the point of view of the victims' families. He just didn't like to express himself strongly. There wasn't a single issue where he didn't see something positive on each side. Now, one could say that he was just being fair-minded. Baloney. I understood a lot more when I met his parents. They were the same way. To them, having a strong opinion was like cursing in church. A definite no-no. Since they were both in their late sixties, I knew there was no hope for them. But Hank was another story. And I had fallen in love with him.

"One night I asked Hank what movie he'd like to see.

" 'You name it.'

" 'Are you interested in a comedy?'

" 'I don't care.'

" 'Action film? Foreign film?'

" 'It doesn't matter.'

" 'But it does, Hank. It really does. It's okay for Charlie, my cat, not to have an opinion, but people must have them. After all, even a Frisbee takes sides.' "

Those words expressed the frustration Abbey was feeling about Hank's indifference. She wasn't looking for an argumentative boyfriend, but with Hank it was like playing tennis with no one on the other side to hit the ball back. She kept repeating the Magic Words, and sure enough, the other day Hank told her that her position on repealing estate taxes was all wrong. She disagreed with him totally, but, as she put it, "Boy, did it ever feel good to have something to disagree over."

Life is all about passion. It's about rooting for your favorite team and for Indiana Jones to get out of the Temple of Doom. Always remember to be polite, but never pull back from stating what you believe.

66

YOU CAN'T TRY AGAIN
UNTIL YOU HANG UP

You keep dialing that number again and again. It's busy. Like a mouse trained to get a food pellet even though it keeps getting shocked, you keep trying. Hey, what gives here? Hurrah, now it's ringing. Finally. But what's this? No one's answering. You hang up and start to dial again, feeling your blood pressure beginning to rise.

It's like all those times you've tried to park your car in a spot that's just a *little* too small to get into. Lots, right? Back up, squeeze in, back up, squeeze in. . . . Finally, you give up—and find a space around the corner that you can get a twelve-wheeler into. Sometimes persistence is the wrong approach. Back off, friend. Put some ice in a glass and then pour in some of your favorite libation. Put your feet up. Read a poem or two (you don't have to write a report on them anymore, so now you can enjoy yourself). Now what was that call all about? Was it really that important? Maybe you should write a letter. Snail mail still works fine for a lot of folks.

Ben's a reporter on a large newspaper. He covers city hall. Sometimes he works for weeks on a long investigative piece. There are always parts of the article that need to be cross-checked or confirmed. But when the people he's interviewed suddenly realize that the article is actually going to run, they start getting nervous. Maybe they've said too much. Ben has learned that if he wants to get more information, he has to stop pushing. He has to back off. He was explaining the problem to us one night over dinner. "You can't try again until you hang up," he said. "If you keep pushing at them, they clam up. So I get very casual, as though it really isn't that important, and I thank them and hang up. I wait a few days, and then I call back. The pressure is off, and they start to talk again."

Ben mentioned the Myth of Sisyphus. "You know, the guy who was fated to push the boulder up the hill for eternity. Well, I've always believed that if ole Sis had stopped a few times while pushing that big boulder up that steep hill, he would have had the extra energy to convince Zeus, or whichever god was running the place, to let him stop. Never forget that backing off doesn't mean giving up. There's a world of difference between the two. We get a lot of busy signals in life. You can't fixate on them. If you put the damn phone down for a while, you'll find that eventually you'll get through."

Ben's Magic Words, "You Can't Try Again Until You Hang Up," taught us the value of backing away from any situation that seems to have reached a dead end. Instead of dissipating our energy and wasting our time listening to busy signals, we hang up, take a break, and try again.

67

AN OLD BROOM GENERALLY
SWEEPS AS WELL AS A NEW ONE

The discovery of a "novelty-seeking gene" clarifies many mysteries of human nature. Both of us know a cadre of people who possess—or rather are afflicted with—the gene, including, we confess, ourselves. Here are a few profiles of carriers:

Tom, a multibillionaire, is the head of a huge corporation. He's an indefatigable pilot who buys the newest Gulfstream as soon as it's on the market. He's a world-class collector of the most cutting-edge art, reads the newest books, sees the latest movies, travels the globe to catch a premiere performance of an opera, frequents little-known museums and galleries, and is a serious gourmet who delights in dining at every new restaurant in the major cities of Europe and the U.S. Not content with the three vast estates he already owns, he's always commissioning the hottest architect to design a new compound in faraway places like the Seychelles, or the tip of Chile. He's so attracted to being around new people and the very newest ideas that he regularly does a clean sweep of his executive roster, replacing his old decision-makers with newer models. He's damaged and even destroyed the lives of highly capable men and women because of his insatiable need for novelty. He's an extreme example of a man in the thrall of the novelty gene.

Now check out Mark. At 29 he's a bungee jumper, races motorcycles, a rock climber who will take on any challenge, and a veteran sky diver. When we met him, he was just about to take on the big waves surfing in Australia—a very dangerous undertaking, as any water sports devotee will tell you. Mark's novelty gene gives him uncontrollable urges to put himself into new and exhilarating—and highly perilous—situations. It also tends to keep him from forming intimate relationships because serious girlfriends back off as soon as it's clear how easily they could end up as widows.

Joelle's novelty gene manifests itself in a slightly different way. She likes new clothes, new jobs, new men, new friends. She follows every fashion trend, casting away the entire contents of her closet twice a year so that everything she wears will be new and up to the minute. As a public relations consultant, she works on a project-by-project basis so that she's never bored by what she's doing—there's always a new client to present her with new challenges. Boyfriends come and go, and friends who thought they were close to her usually find themselves replaced by a new chum or a new inner circle.

The novelty gene has many very positive aspects. It gives you a strong sense of curiosity and a desire to educate yourself and to expand your life through new and interesting challenges and adventures. It can lead you to seek out new people and exciting new ideas. Both of us possess a mutation of the novelty gene. We certainly thrive on new experiences, new places, new concepts, new people. But, unlike the folks above, we're aware too much novelty can be a dangerous thing. Lasting relationships are the key to a rich, well-lived life. Tom never keeps executives around long enough to benefit from their experience and in-depth knowledge of his business. Joelle never takes enough time with people to see what they're really about.

Her relationships are exciting, sure, but they're also very superficial. And Mark, the big wave rider—we predict that one day his fixation on new, over-the-top adventures that keep him from deep personal attachments will probably result in serious injury. Even worse, all three are hurting others with their constant drive for the next big thing.

The great news is that we're not totally at the mercy of our genetic heritage. The influence of our genes can be modified. We can transform our behavior, leaving behind our old, damaging habits. If someone you care about is in thrall to the dark side of the novelty gene, or if you have been a victim of a "clean sweep," we suggest you try these Magic Words: "An Old Broom Generally Sweeps as Well as a New One." A high-quality broom, well crafted and well designed, may have some dings and dents and a few frayed edges, but it's capable of years of service.

68

IT'S NOT THE CURE FOR CANCER

Four months after graduating from Stanford, Michelle, the smart, aggressive, and very attractive daughter of a mutual friend of ours, had worked her way from an assistant researcher to an associate reporter at one of America's largest newsweeklies. She fervently chased stories and filed more articles than the two other beat reporters combined. She worked tirelessly, and on Friday, the night each issue went to press, she stayed at the office until dawn. (She was not required to do so.) Most weekends she was at her desk, surfing the Net for news items and possible leads. One Sunday her boss, who happened to be in the office, stopped by her desk and remarked, "Michelle, everybody can see you're doing a fine job, but remember, you need a life, this is not the cure for cancer." Michelle, pleased to be noticed, was surprised at the comment and laughed as if her boss had made a joke.

Michelle was young and loved the business. But, like all industries, magazines have their ups and downs. A few months after Michelle arrived, the economy took a nosedive. Advertising was down and circulation was beginning to sag. The higher-ups called for a redesign of the magazine as they renewed their efforts to beat their rivals. The pressure to perform was intense. Editors and reporters battled the competition—and each other—for news.

Michelle thrived in this cutthroat environment. She was soon spotted by a high-profile, well-financed dot-com company that was planning to launch a multimillion-dollar website in conjunction with a new print magazine. They offered her a position as senior editor, and the signing package included stock options, perks, and an attractive salary plus a hefty bonus. Michelle jumped at it.

A start-up is a different kind of brutal. The hours and effort Michelle was putting in made her previous job look like a walk in the park. One weekend, after eight months working herself to the max, Michelle was completely wiped out. She spent the entire weekend in bed, climbing out only to make some soup and down a couple of pieces of cheese with Saltines.

What was she doing with her life? She was too tired to even think about it.

On Monday she was back at her desk, delivering the goods with her usual intensity. The premiere issue was going to press in three days, and to say that the entire staff was stressed and edgy would be a major understatement. Michelle dug in even harder, wanting to score big points with a last-minute super-scoop that she'd been working on for months.

She had delayed a trip to the ladies' room for over an hour to make phone calls, and when she finally walked down the hall to the bathroom, some barely perceptible sounds echoed in her mind, "My god, I don't even take the time to pee anymore. What am I doing? *This is not the cure for cancer.*"

She returned to her cubicle, phoned the deli for her usual no-fat yogurt and Diet Coke lunch, and sat back with her heels propped on the edge of her desk. Suddenly, her former boss's words meant something to her. She was not in a life and death race against a deadly disease or on the verge of an epoch-making discovery. She was not tracking down the AIDS virus, trying to crack the human genome, or working to eradicate Alzheimer's. She was a journalist—a damn good one—doing her job. Suddenly, everything came into perspective. A career is something you work hard at. If you love what you're doing, you do it with energy and smarts and passion. But it's not worth ruining your life—or your kidneys—over.

Michelle put on her coat, planning to take a walk around the block. Sushi Yasuda, a three-star restaurant, was a few doors from her office. Although she loved Japanese food, she'd never been in the place. She walked through its doors, into a quiet, high-ceilinged space done in pale woods, and asked if she could be seated even though she had no reservation.

Luckily, they had a table for her. She settled herself, perused the elegant menu, and ordered a cold sake. She couldn't remember the last time she'd had a glass of wine or a drink at lunch, or even a Bloody Mary on the weekend. For the next hour she sipped her sake and enjoyed the superb sushi.

Being privy to Michelle's exhausting work pattern, you might be tempted to predict that the newfound perspective the Magic Words had given to her would last a few hours or a few days and then give way to old habits. But the expression truly worked magic. Michelle still worked hard, but her point of view had completely changed. A man she had dated casually turned out to be potential husband material once she made up her mind to spend more time with him. She now answered her friends' e-mails, returned their calls, watered her plants, and even signed up for Saturday-morning drawing classes.

Take a woman who prides herself on keeping her house spotless and orderly. You can eat off the floors, ogle the amazing organization of every closet, appreciate the gloss on each of the dozens of objects in the many rooms, be astounded by the appliances that have been there for twenty years but look brand-new. This woman is consumed by housekeeping. She's lost her perspective on dirt—and life. It's not the cure for cancer, it's just a house she's taking care of. Surely she would get more out of living by taking our Magic Words to heart. Do her—or any other person obsessed over something that's not so important in the big scheme of things—a big, big favor. Make them take a time-out, sit down—preferably over a cup of coffee (make it decaf)—and tell them the Magic Words. You'll see how they succeed in refocusing a person on what's important in life.

Back to Michelle, to date she's dropped the art classes, but she's working pretty steadily on the romantic relationship. In another job switch, she's become editor in chief of a small magazine that has the promise of becoming a major one. We're sure she'll take it to the top, but we're also positive that she knows "It's Not the Cure for Cancer" . . . although we're hoping she gets the scoop on that story someday very soon.

69

CAN YOU SAVE IT?

"Hey Marge, what's up?"

"Oh, the usual, I have an early meeting, and I'm trying to dash out the door—"

"I just have to tell you what happened last night. Charlie and I had a huge fight about the dog."

"Was it a serious fight? Or just the same old argument about whether you should get a Briard or a Scottie?"

"Well, it escalated into a fight over who does what around the house. I know I'd have to take care of the dog and end up walking it three times a day. I really am sick and tired of him sitting in front of the TV and watching his programs. Last night the dishes just sat in the sink—and he knows damn well he's supposed to do them. And I wasn't going to nag. It just drives me crazy—"

"Marge, I know this is important, but we've gotta talk about this later. I'm going to be late for this meeting—"

"Just give me another minute."

Sue, being a good friend, continues to press the receiver to her ear as she flicks the finishing touches on her mascara.

"So I'm thinking we'd better see a couples counselor—" Marge continues.

"I hate to do this, but I've got to hang up, Marge, I'm really going to be late—"

"Just let me finish this thought..."

We know a few Marges, and you probably do too—in our book, Marge has a benign but common syndrome: she's a certified phone-aholic. This amazingly annoying condition includes these symptoms:

Love of making phone calls

Repeated use of the telephone

Irresistible urge to check in with friends at least once a day

Inability to hang up

Need to control length of conversation

Sue will tell you that Marge is a wonderful friend and a lovable person. Even though they are truly close, Sue is uncomfortable about confronting Marge about her Phone Problem. No matter how hard—or how diplomatically—Sue tries to end a conversation, Marge always adds, "Just give me a second..." or "This will only take another minute..."

Marge is surrounded by family and friends, and yet, for whatever reason, she finds it necessary to rack up huge phone bills each month. There's another category of phone-aholic, the lonely caller. These are men and women who often spend their days alone and need to make human contact, so they pick up the receiver and are unwilling to put it down. Both types cause problems for the person on the other end of the line.

When dealing with a lonely caller, it's helpful to start out with "I love hearing your voice..." or "Great to talk to you."

This transmits the feeling that you haven't forgotten about them and makes the person feel less alone. If you're dealing with a garden-variety type like Marge, your voice should sound rushed and harried, and you should immediately begin to ease into the hang-up with words like the following:

"I'm on my way out the door . . ."

"I'm in the middle of doing something . . ."

"My cell phone is buzzing and I've got to get it . . ."

"Someone's ringing the doorbell . . ."

You can quickly go from the ease-out into the hang-up with the Magic Words, "Gotta go . . . *can you save it?*"

Ninety-nine times out of a hundred the person will forget what was so important that he or she absolutely had to keep you on the phone. When they inevitably call again, start the conversation by saying, "Last time we talked [then add sweetly but pointedly, "this morning," "yesterday," "a half-hour ago"] you wanted to tell me something—what was it?" We bet they won't even know what it was that was so important. And when they begin to yammer endlessly once again, use the Magic Words, and remember that you don't ever have to feel guilty about getting off the phone—and giving yourself a break.

70

NOW OR NEVER?
GIVE US A BREAK!

"Now or Never" are truly Magic Words—of the sort we don't recommend. They can make things vanish—a lover, a job, a friend, an opportunity. Whenever we think about using these potentially dangerous Magic Words, we add a parenthetical caution as a reminder that ultimatums are to life what hot peppers are to stew. Used sparingly, they may be exactly what's needed. Thrown in by the handful, they can ruin everything.

Having said that, we both agree that there are times when ultimatums are necessary, and we write about that in the section titled "When You Draw the Line, Do It in Cement."

But here we're talking about how to deal with people who use ultimatums to control you. "Now or Never" people are trouble. We try to get them to ease off with "Give us a break!" If that doesn't work, we put them out of our lives.

That's why we no longer go to the movies with Jill. The first time we opened the *Times* to the movie page and began to consider what we all might like to see, we were amused when Jill said, "If we can't see *Life Is Beautiful,* I don't want to go." We wanted to see that film, too, so we gave in to her request. (We were naive enough then to think of it as a request.) But several films and several ultimatums later, we were no longer amused.

Most ultimatums are about larger things. Jerry came to work for Alice, a friend of ours, because he had gotten tired of receiving ultimatums from his boss. The man had begun to make a habit of handing Jerry work on Friday afternoon and asking him to finish it by Monday. When, on the third such occasion, Jerry protested that he had plans for the weekend, his boss offered his own version of "Now or Never." "Well, let me put it this way. Which would you rather do—finish it this weekend or find another job?"

Jerry went along; he had to. But when he heard through the grapevine that Alice was looking for help, he picked up the phone and called. He told us later that he didn't give notice immediately after Alice hired him. He waited until Friday, when his boss handed him the file folder. Once more he meekly protested that he had plans for the weekend. The boss did what Jerry knew he'd do. He issued the ultimatum, and this time Jerry repeated it, "Finish it this weekend or find another job?" Then Jerry said that he handed back the file folder and announced, "I guess I'll find another job."

Remembering the look on that man's face, said Jerry, would give him pleasure for the rest of his life.

When friends try to dictate your decisions, try the Magic Words, "Now or Never? Give Me a Break!" If that fails to budge them from their controlling ways, don't stick around. When you're dealing with people who play a central role in your life—an employer or a mate—the Magic Words may have to be said silently as a mantra to be followed in the future. They'll remind you that if the situation can't be changed, you'd better think of leaving it. One day, when the demand is "Now or Never," you may respond with "Never."

71

IT'S A ROUGH PATCH IN
THE LONG ROAD OF LIFE

A woman we know wears a golden ring with a mysterious hieroglyph on it. We've never seen her without it on her finger, so we asked her where it was from and what it meant to her.

"I bought this in Egypt from a very old man who told me that it was a ring to be worn for the rest of my life. He said that I should look at it in bad times because they would pass. But he was emphatic that I should also gaze at the ring in good times, because they too would pass."

All lives have their ups and downs, but Sarah was having a really tough time. Her marriage was on the rocks, she'd been laid off from her part-time teaching job, and she felt snowed under with money troubles. Not only that, her two children had recurrent cases of mono, and her mother had died a few months previously. It was becoming increasingly clear that her father couldn't live alone, and since she was an only child, she'd have to find an assisted-living facility and help him to move in. The last straw was that her much-loved Chesapeake retriever had been hit and killed by a car. There seemed to be no end to the troubles in her life.

Sarah had always been an easygoing, upbeat person, and when a close pal of hers, Lisa, saw her at a large cocktail party,

Sarah seemed exactly the way she had always been—serene and smiling. Lisa thought Sarah must have had some pretty good acting lessons. The next morning, Lisa got to thinking about all that was happening to her dear friend. Even though she appeared to be in pretty good shape on the surface, she must be really suffering down deep. Lisa decided to treat her to a nice lunch and see if there was anything she or her husband could do to help.

Since the kids were not feeling well again, and they were home from school (again), Lisa brought some fancy sandwiches over to Sarah's place. She told her she knew all the stuff Sarah was coping with and asked how could she make her life a bit easier. Could she stay with the kids, bring casseroles, make calls about her father? What did Sarah need? Lisa and her husband, Sam, were ready to pitch in immediately.

Sarah was so grateful for her friend's generous offer that tears of gratitude welled in her eyes.

"For a few weeks, I cried and cried," Sarah told Lisa, "then I ranted and raved. Then I got so angry at everybody and everything I couldn't see straight. I was just in a rage against the universe for handing out so much shit."

"But," interrupted Lisa, "you seem fine on the outside. How are you managing?"

"Now I really am fine. It took some time, but I realized that *it's only a rough patch in the long road of life.* Different things work for different people. I can't really explain why, but just saying those words loud and clear gets me through each day."

Lisa thought a great deal about Sarah's Magic Words. She remembered the woman who had worn the ring with the glyph on it. She bought a small locket for Sarah and had it engraved with the phrase *"It's only a rough patch. . . ."* Even though the bad times are long since over, Sarah refuses to take off her locket.

These are Magic Words you can say to anyone who's facing a constellation of difficult circumstances. Life, as we've heard it said so often, is a long, winding road. You never know what the next curve will bring, a beautiful panorama or a dangerous pothole. One thing is certain, as long as you're alive you're still moving forward, and eventually you'll leave the obstacles behind. Paste the Magic Words on your mental windshield as a reminder that unwelcome detours finally do end, and easier stretches lie ahead.

72

I NEED YOUR HELP

These words are really and truly magical in their persuasive powers. We heard them from a legendary publishing executive whose reputation rests on getting what she wants—against any and all odds.

The reason *"I need your help"* works so beautifully is that it's difficult to say no to someone who comes right out and asks for your assistance. A simple "I need help" doesn't cut it, the word "your" is what gives the phrase clout because the words become personal. "Can you help me?" is also unmagical, as it is a question, and the person can easily respond with a "No."

Suppose you're stuck with a hideous AT&T bill. You've been charged for calls to Timbuktu, and you've been on the phone for hours trying to straighten it out. Your frustration level has risen to heart-attack proportions, and you want to shriek at the person on the other end of the line. Instead of open warfare with the phone company, try taking a very deep breath and saying "I really need your help on this." You'll find, nine times out of ten, that the person on the other end of the line changes their tune and tries to lend a hand. Better yet, at the beginning of your call, start out with a sweet "I need your help." If aid is not forthcoming, ask to speak to the supervisor—these Magic Words are very effective on those in charge.

"I need your help" comes in handy when people really don't want to be helpful. Take a difficult co-worker, for example. You need her to be cooperative on a project, and you know in advance she'll say, "I can't do that." Try the Magic Words, and see how hard it is for her to turn you down. Another example, closer to home: instead of haranguing your husband or wife with "You never do the dishes," "You never do the shopping," "You never clean up the baby's messes," reverse your tactics and use the Magic Words. Even the most intractable spouse is willing to give you a hearing—and maybe even a hand—when you ask for assistance. Keep in mind in hardened domestic situations that a warm smile—instead of the usual bleat—will also support your cause.

Medical situations are another area where these Magic Words can work wonders. Over and over we hear of doctors who rush patients out of their offices, surgeons who are chilly and can't be bothered with answering crucial questions, nurses who are overworked and have no time to spare. "I need your help" is the kind of phrase that reminds harried or callous professionals they're dealing with humans, not cases on a computer.

Our legendary publishing executive cites a super-effective variation of her Magic Words: *"You're the only person who can help me."* This ratchets up the seduction potential of the phrase and flatters the person who is being asked for something. Play this back to yourself: someone calls you on the phone and says "You're the only person who can help me" . . . what's your reaction? That the person is using you? Probably not. That you are special, and you have talents that could be put to good use? More likely.

We put these Magic Words in our top ten because they're so valuable in a myriad of situations. Use them, you'll find they have true power.

73

WASHING DIRTY LINEN
SHOULD ONLY BE DONE
IN THE LAUNDROMAT

Andy, who's a lawyer in Tucson, told us this story:

"I went through a sad experience a few years ago. It was the kind of thing that makes you squirm in your seat when you see it in a movie. I had been dating Carla, a paralegal in our office, for a few months. I had vowed never to become involved with someone from the office, but Carla seemed to be special. First off, she was extremely attractive and had an upbeat personality. She also possessed a ton of energy and focus and was preparing to go to school at night to become a lawyer.

"One day I was working late. The office was deserted. I went down to the small kitchen on our floor for a cup of coffee. I was about to walk in when I heard two women talking and laughing. One of them was Carla. What she said next stopped me in my tracks.

" 'I don't think you were working here when Vince was in the office,' I heard Carla say to the other woman. 'He was a litigator and real smart. We dated for almost six months. Vince was easily my number one experience in speed sex. This guy generally had an orgasm before he had a chance to take his socks off.' (Laughter from both of them here.) 'Of course, it upset him a lot. But what about me? I guess it's nice not having sex take up all your time, but give me a break! The only thing we shared sexually was talking about it.' (More laughter)

"I slink back to my office," Andy said, finishing the story, "so that Carla and the other woman wouldn't know what I had heard. I remained friendly with Carla, but you don't have to be a psychic to know that I never dated her again."

We all have dirty secrets. We all have nasty tales to tell. We all know lots of things we'd just as soon forget. But why do we sometimes bring out this junk as if it were a Fabergé egg inherited from our grandparents? There's something in most of us that likes to hear this kind of gossip, and worse, to pass it on. Believe me, if we weren't willing to hear it, it wouldn't be told.

The next time someone comes to you to air their dirty laundry, shut off the gossip with a joke if you can, but even if you have to sound like a prude, make it clear that you're not interested in life's tawdry tales. With most people, it's probably enough to merely think the Magic Words—"Washing Dirty Linen Should Only Be Done in the Laundromat"—to remind yourself to change the subject. Dishing dirt requires someone to listen as well as someone to talk. But some people are such insistent gossipers that you may have to say the Magic Words out loud. Don't worry about hurting their feelings. They aren't worrying about anyone else's.

74

HOW CAN WE SPLIT UP IF WE HAVEN'T EVEN STARTED YET?

We've known Amy and Fred for a long time. Actually, we were the ones who introduced them to each other. They shared so many common interests and traits that we thought they would be a natural couple. And at first we were right.

They both loved sports and were always playing tennis or going to basketball games. Amy enjoyed cooking and Fred liked to eat. They both enjoyed movies and would see at least one a week. They were talking about living together when they suddenly split up. We couldn't understand it, and, interestingly, neither could they. Was it a blowup? No. Unfaithfulness? No. Let's hear it from them.

Amy: "The funny thing was that we never had a big fight. No slamming of doors, no long periods of giving each other the silent treatment. Nothing like that. He had some habits that irritated me. Small, annoying stuff. Like drinking out of the juice container while standing in front of the fridge. Or not turning off the TV when I was talking to him. But there was much more that I liked. Fred was affectionate and easygoing. He cared about people and was constantly trying to help his friends out. He was, in the best sense of the term, a nice guy.

Then one day, one of us—I don't even remember who—said something like 'maybe we should try being apart for a while.' And that's what we did."

Fred: "I liked Amy a lot. I even used the 'L' word with her, and that's how I felt. She could be a little overbearing at times. Sort of schoolmarmish. 'Make sure you take an umbrella, it might rain,' or 'Don't you think you eat a bit too much junk food? You'll pay for it someday.' It didn't drive me crazy, but I didn't like it. I was, however, crazy about the way Amy looked and smelled. Still am. And she had a good sense of humor. I don't know how many times we would see something while walking on the street, and we'd both start laughing at the exact same time. It was really great. I remember that she was the one who thought we should split up for a bit. I'm pretty sure of it. I still don't know why we did it. You know, when you open a door and walk out it's sometimes real hard to open it and go back in. I guess that's why we never got back together."

Amy and Fred broke up because of a list of petty complaints and irritations that taken together didn't amount to much—at least not in our eyes. The real problem was that they just wouldn't hang in there a while longer. They didn't give the relationship a chance, and, as a result, they broke up before they ever got started—something we still think was a big mistake.

Sometimes when a couple splits up it's a positive thing. The two people got together for the wrong reasons, and the relationship is proving harmful to both of them. Then it's right to end it. But you don't get rid of a new car when a windshield-wiper blade breaks. You don't throw a new suit away when a button falls off. The beginnings of relationships are a lot like diving into a pool early in the morning. At first it might be a bit chilly, but if you do a couple of laps you'll find the temperature is just fine. Give the other person as much of a chance as you'd give to yourself. You should never split up until you've given the relationship the opportunity to at least have a decent start.

75

WHAT DO YOU KNOW
THAT I DON'T KNOW?

Rumor has it that when a top TV personality, admired for her looks and smarts, is at a swank party she softly says to her dinner partner, *"Tell me something intimate about yourself."* Talk about leading questions!

Her approach got us to thinking about other seductive come-ons. Long ago, when Alexandra was researching her bestsellers on love and sex, one of the men she interviewed provided a line that we feel deserves Magic Word status.

Steve was a great believer in romance as the way to a woman's heart and body. He would pursue the object of his desire with elegant candlelight dinners that he cooked himself, complete with champagne and caviar. The next morning he would send a dozen roses or a small bottle of perfume selected especially for his current amour. All this highly focused attention, he reported, achieved amazingly successful results.

When Alexandra asked what kind of woman appealed to him, he took a long moment to reflect.

"It's not about body type for me," he replied. "She has to like herself, and she has to love sex."

"How can you tell if she 'loves' sex?"

"It's not so easy to describe. For me the signals can be in

the clothes she wears—silky, soft stuff—the way she touches you, her responses to sexual hints . . ."

"Has a woman ever surprised you in bed?"

"Women," he answered, "are always surprising. Obviously, that's part of the appeal. There was one particular woman who really caught my attention. She wasn't beautiful at all. But there was something about her—"

"Tell me about that 'something.' "

"We'd been seeing each other for a month or two, and one night when we were lying in bed, she asked me, 'What do you know that I don't know?' It blew me away. It was one of the sexiest things a woman ever said to me."

"Why is that?"

"There was stuff I wanted to explore, and I really didn't know how to bring it up. That was the perfect lead-in and a huge turn-on."

When you think about that woman's question for a few seconds, you'll probably agree that it is a very sexy technique for unlocking reticence and reserve. Being totally free with each other is one of the keys to terrific sex. Whether you're first-time lovers or have been married for years, the question brings up the issue of experiencing or doing something new—another source of great sex, especially in a long-term relationship, where things can tend to get a little routine. It doesn't matter which partner's doing the asking or the answering. "What Do You Know That I Don't Know?" is a no-fail magic question.

76

THAT'S MORE THAN
I CARE TO KNOW

"My daughter—you've met her, haven't you?—is dating this man who's five years younger than she is. He's trying to be a rock star. How do you get to be a rock star, anyway? Well, she's been seeing him for two months, and it turns out he has gonorrhea—"

"Lynn, I've never met your daughter, and that is just a bit more than I care to know."

"So I've got about $50,000 in debt, and my credit cards are maxed. My mother forced me to see this financial planner, who told me I had to pay down the credit cards each month, $150 on the Visa, $85 on the MasterCard, $65 on the Diner's Club—and it's killing me!"

"Hey Harry, that's really more than I care to know."

"My husband started seeing this other woman, and I found out about it. I went ballistic. Because, let me tell you, when we were in bed something just wasn't working, if you know what I mean—"

"Really, Marge, that's more than I care to know."

You're cornered at a party, on the phone, in a business situation, or sitting by the pool when you're on vacation, and someone begins to dump embarrassing personal information on you. A marvelous "steel magnolia" from San Antonio named Louise uses this show-stopping phrase—*"Dear, that's more than I care to know"*—to cut off the flow of unwanted data. People—and they might even be close friends—can overload your circuits with too much detail, or something you definitely should not hear or do not want any part of. This is the moment to say the Magic Words, nicely—but firmly. They allow you to continue the conversation in a less intimate way—or to end it altogether.

77

MY BEING ON TIME REALLY
REQUIRES YOUR HELP

Have you ever run a three-legged race? If so, you know that it's not that easy. Winning the race requires some practice. To get to the finish line first (and together), you need to take into account the other person's abilities and practice beforehand. A team made up of two people with normal abilities who have practiced will most likely defeat any team that has not, even if the other team includes an Olympic track star. Teamwork is the key.

Now what does this have to do with being on time? Very little, when it comes to one person's ability to be punctual. But when you're involved in being on time with another person, say a spouse, it becomes a much more complicated issue. Our friend Jocelyn had a lot of grief with this problem until some Magic Words came to the rescue.

"I'm both a neatnik and a maniac when it comes to being on time. Maybe the two things are related. I've been that way since I was a kid. A lot of people couldn't believe it when Doug and I started to live together. They thought our relationship would last minutes, not years. He is always late. His mother even told me that she's convinced she was in labor for twenty hours because Doug wanted to establish himself as one of the tardiest guys on the planet.

"When you love someone you tend to overlook certain traits that are annoying, thinking that in time the other person will change. Over the years Doug has made some strides. He's become somewhat less of a slob. I've actually gotten him to put his dirty clothes in the hamper. This was like establishing peace in the Middle East. It took a *ton* of work. On the other hand, I've been totally unable to help Doug overcome his chronic lateness.

"Whenever we have to go somewhere together I'm forced to run on his clock, which means we can be forty-five minutes, even an hour late for dinner parties. It drives me crazy. Since living with Doug, I've mellowed slightly, but his lateness is just plain rudeness as far as I'm concerned, and I'll never mellow out that much. I tried sitting him down and pleading my case in a careful and persuasive manner. Doug nodded and smiled at me. I would see a change in him, he vowed. Just give him a little more time.

"There was no improvement. In fact, his lateness became worse. What really bothered me was that Doug was perfectly capable of being on time if it really mattered to *him*. In business, he's pretty much always on time. If he has tickets to a football game, he's in his seat before the kickoff. When it suits him, he's Johnny-on-the-spot. That's what makes me nuts. Sitting at dinner one night, I explained all this, and said, " 'My being on time really requires your help.

" 'If I can't get your help, I'm going to run completely on my own clock. That means when we have a dinner party to go to at eight, I'm going to be there at eight. I might be the first to arrive, but that doesn't bother me. I like arriving on time.

I'm tired of showing up late everywhere because I'm yoked to your lateness. You can arrive at whatever time you choose. Is that okay with you, dear?'

" 'You mean we're not going to friends' houses together?'

" 'We are, Doug, but we're going together separately. It's making me too crazy to wait around for you, and I can't see that you're enjoying this much either.

"I'd love to tell you that the Magic Words changed Doug overnight. It would have been great if he suddenly went from D.S.T. (Doug Standard Time) to everyone's time. It didn't happen that way. He went from being an hour late to forty-five minutes late—for him, a big improvement. Right now we're at the thirty-minute mark, and I'm pretty pleased about it. Will he someday arrive at a dinner party together with me? All I know is that I'm not going to stop saying "My Being on Time Really Requires Your Help" until it happens. So far, so good."

78

HEY! YOU'RE STANDING
ON MY FOOT

Our friend Blair gave us these Magic Words a few years back, and it's surprising how frequently we use them. First, a word about Blair. She's in her early forties and has been married for ten years. Both she and her husband, Andre, teach high school. She's smart and has a wicked sense of humor that only comes out after she gets to know a person well. That's because Blair is a little shy. Actually, that's not really accurate. Blair is VERY shy, and it took us quite a while to get to know her. So these Magic Words are particularly well suited for folks who have a retiring nature. Folks who sometimes have trouble dealing with certain overly aggressive types and wish there were Magic Words that would make them disappear.

Blair described how these words originated.

"I always seem to get cornered at parties by people, generally men, who stand too close and talk too loudly—usually about subjects that only they find interesting. I guess since I basically have a quiet nature, these loud guys love it when they find a person like me. 'Ah,' their subconscious says to them, 'you've found the perfect audience. Pour it on.' I hate to be rude, so I always feign interest as this superego postures and pontificates in my face. I nod my head occasionally and keep a small smile locked in place as Mr. Charm rambles through his complete, boring repertoire. It used to be that I couldn't extract myself from these painful situations until the bore finally ran out of energy, sort of like a child's windup toy winding down.

"Over dinner one night I was telling my brother, Benjy, about a particularly painful experience I had had the night before, when I was cornered by a man I'll call The Accountant from Hell. This jerk automatically assumed that I wanted to hear every detail of the recent changes in the state's tax code. He was extremely proud that the state senator in charge of the committee that rewrote the code was a fraternity brother of his! I gently tried to get off the subject, but only a stick of dynamite could have dislodged him.

"'Why didn't you do what you used to do to Uncle Teddy?'

"'What are you talking about?' I asked Benjy.

"'Don't you remember that when you were a little kid, you couldn't stand it when Uncle Teddy would grab you up and plop you down on his lap. He had a real loud voice and breath that could peel paint. Only Mom, his adoring sister, could see Teddy's charms. To get away from him, you'd tell him he was standing on your foot. He'd answer, "You're sitting on my lap, Blair, darling. How could I be standing on your foot?" "Well, something is hurting me, Uncle Teddy." He'd laugh, and while he was distracted you'd grab the chance to slip away.'

"And right there I finally had the Magic Words that I needed to escape these painful situations. Now, when I'm cornered, I say, 'Hey! You're standing on my foot.' Invariably, the man who's been lecturing stops talking and looks down. Then they always say, 'I'm not standing on your foot.' But it's too late. While they looked down, I slipped away."

What we love about Blair's Magic Words is that they work

for all those people who are too shy or too kind to bat away life's bores. The person who hears them is never hurt, merely confused, and too busy wondering exactly what happened to renew the conversational attack. And, for a change, those who are gentle and shy get to have a guiltless good time.

79

A FEW GOOD FRIENDS MAKE
YOU VERY POPULAR

Both of us have heavy-duty Rolodexes. We're quite proud of them. We don't need a forklift to move them yet, but they're getting there. Every year, just to keep them manageable, we do a thorough culling. Out go the folks who've passed away (never an easy thing to do) and those who have otherwise moved out of our lives. That still leaves a lot of people. Recently, one of us asked the other, looking at one of these sumo-wrestler-sized Rolodexes: "How many of the people in there do you think are good friends of yours?"

"A lot" was the automatic reply.

"Take a second to think that over. What I'm talking about is the kind of good friend you can call at 3 A.M. with worries and insecurities, or just for a good cry. The kind of person who'll put their life on hold while they deal with a problem in yours. That's what I mean by a good friend."

After a little more thought and a long discussion we both knew the real answer. Damn few. It's those few good friends that define and amplify our lives, and though it's nice to know a lot of people and better yet to be friendly with a good number of them, true good friends are the most important component in a happy life.

Ben, an old friend of ours who works in advertising and is a world-class schmoozer, fell for Cindy, a lawyer he met at a friend's dinner party. They started seeing each other almost every night. Within a few months they were talking about living together. But there was one thing about Ben that bothered Cindy. She loved the fact that he knew lots of people and seemed to like most of them, but she couldn't stand the way that he called everyone "my good friend." Almost every introduction was prefaced by "Cindy, I want to introduce you to my really good friend . . ." It wasn't easy, but it annoyed her so much she decided to talk to Ben about it. Cindy felt strongly that Ben's use of this phrase was wrong and, even worse, phony.

"Ben, dear, we've been together for a while, and it's been good." This immediately elicited a kiss from Ben, who added, "No, it's been very good." This, of course, made it tougher for Cindy to say what she wanted to, but after a moment she soldiered on. "Why do you call everyone your good friend? Sometimes you say that about a person you've only met a couple of times." Ben was quiet for a while before he answered.

"Do I really do that?"

"Yes, constantly."

"Why does it bother you?"

Cindy explained to him that good friends are truly important—certainly hers were—and that since we have so few of them, to lump them in with almost everyone else diminished their worth.

The next day Ben said to her that he had given it a lot of thought, and he felt that Cindy was right. He made a list of who his good friends truly were, and he wasn't even able to get up to ten. It stunned him.

"That there were so few?" she asked.

"Yes, but more importantly that I've never realized before how important they are to me."

Ben now refers to people he knows as 1) good friends, 2) people he's friendly with, and 3) acquaintances. And as Ben now says, "A Few Good Friends Make You Very Popular."

80

DON'T FORGET YOU'RE NOT IN A TELEPHONE BOOTH!

This is about cell phones. Like the pods in the movie *Invasion of the Body Snatchers,* they're everywhere. Recently one of us was in a crowded elevator in a large office building. As the elevator descended it made a stop, and a young, well-dressed woman stepped in. Everybody shifted a bit to make room for her. The woman was talking on her cell phone and didn't pause for a moment. Here's what she said: "I disagree with you, Jan. I really do. I've thought about this a lot. I mean an awful lot. I'm going to do it. Yes, I'm sure it's the right thing to do. Well, I don't care that Donna agrees with you. I've already made the appointment. Day after tomorrow, I'm going to have the abortion." The people in the tightly packed elevator let out a collective gasp. How could someone say something as personal as that in an elevator full of strangers?

The latest-model cell phones are smaller and cuter than ever before, and people are bellowing into them everywhere we turn. Want to hear the intimate details of someone's finances, love life, job prospects, mental state, or drinking problem? Want to hear things that would make a priest blush in confessional? Just walk behind or stand next to one of the myriad cell chatterers marching up and down the streets and avenues of our country. (It's even worse abroad, but at least there you can't understand what's being said.) Remember when, not that long ago, people went into a phone booth to make a PERSONAL call and closed the door behind them? Phone booths are not going to make a big comeback, but manners and respect for others still have a chance.

Stan is a good friend of ours who lives in Des Moines. He came up with the Magic Words we're using here and has also devised a strategy for dealing with cell phone abusers. This one is really quite simple. Whenever he's seated next to someone on a train or bus who's yakking away on a cell phone, he opens the book or magazine he has with him and starts to *read aloud*. When the person next to him looks over, he says, "I'm ready to stop whenever you are. I do prefer to read to myself, but you know how it is." He reports that this works almost all the time, though once he was forced to read half of a *Newsweek* magazine aloud.

We have a confession to make: we both have cell phones. Our rule on making calls is simple: stop and move into a doorway or some other private spot, and, in a normal voice, make your call. If we have to shout for the other person to hear, we end the call and make it later. And just the way we automatically hold a door open for the person behind us, the one who keeps the phone on will *always* turn it off whenever entering a room, office, or restaurant. Pretty simple, isn't it?

A cell phone is great when you're running late or your car has broken down. But how many of the conversations we hear shouted out on the street are that important? Judging by what we've heard, damn few. There's really nothing worse than listening to someone yak about petty personal problems, so next time you're forced to listen to a lot more than you care to know, lean toward the offender and say, "Don't Forget You're NOT in a Telephone Booth."

81

I LIKE TO DANCE, BUT CAN'T
WE TAKE TURNS LEADING?

Who would dispute that it takes two to tango? We love to watch world-class ballroom dancers swirl around the dance floor with a grace that appears to be effortless. Of course, we know that long hours of practice have gone into the three-minute dance number. And though the man is always leading his female partner, you can be assured that the two of them have carefully worked out every step, twirl, and pause in their routine. So, in effect, they are both leading.

Dancers achieve success because each knows how to respond to the subtle signals the other gives. In all good relationships, people have learned to do the same.

When our friend Sandy married Geoff, she inherited Wayne. Wayne and Geoff had been roommates in college and good friends ever since. When, several years after their marriage, Sandy and Geoff planned a trip to Egypt, they asked Wayne if he'd like to come along. Wayne offered to make the arrangements, and, without consulting the couple, he scheduled their itinerary, chose when and where they'd eat their meals, and even worked out time slots for museums and shopping. Sandy and Geoff didn't want to spoil the trip, so they tried joking about the way Wayne had regimented the holiday. Geoff developed a snappy salute that he offered up whenever Wayne began pushing them to keep to the schedule. Sandy moaned that she was tired of seeing Egypt in double time; could they have one day to dawdle? Wayne didn't take the hints. After they were home, the three met for dinner, and Geoff said that if they were to travel together again, it might be better if everyone involved had more say in the planning.

"I thought things went really well," Wayne responded, an edge to his voice. "Didn't you enjoy the trip?"

"Of course we did. And your planning is perfect," Geoff soothed. "But that was the problem. It was too perfect. Less like a vacation and more like the D day invasion. How do we know how much time we should spend in a museum before we've even seen it?"

"Yes, well all right," said Wayne, and shortly afterward he announced that he wasn't feeling well and would have to go home.

You don't have to be a tarot reader to know that this conversation marked Wayne's last trip with Geoff and Sandy. Several days later Wayne called to say that the following summer he'd be taking a holiday with someone else. Wayne wasn't willing to dance unless everyone followed his lead.

Bernie, who runs a Volvo dealership, does the same thing. A few months after he'd moved to Seattle, Bernie mentioned to one of his salesmen that he loved poker and missed his regular game. The next day the salesman invited him to a weekly game held at the house of a local banker. Bernie knew only one other person in the game, the employee who had invited him.

As each player took his turn dealing, he announced the game as five-card stud. When it was Bernie's turn to deal, he said, "The game will be seven card, high-low, deuces in the hole wild."

"We don't play that, Bernie," said one of the other players.

"Why not?"

"Because most of us don't like it."

"It's dealer's choice," said Bernie, slapping the cards down in front of each player. "One . . . two. . . . three . . . four . . . five . . . six . . . seven. . . . who's in?"

The rest of the players picked up their cards, but no one met Bernie's eyes. One by one they threw their chips in the pot. For the rest of the evening, everyone at the table dealt five-card stud except Bernie, who persisted in calling for "seven card, high-low, deuces in the hole wild." A newcomer, he refused to make any effort to fit in and failed to read the signals the other players sent.

Bernie exercised dealer's choice, but so did the rest of the group. They got together and voted Bernie out. Bernie's not a bad person; he just hasn't learned to give up control. In life we all encounter people who are determined to have their way. Bullheaded, they rarely accept direct criticism, but many will allow you to tease them out of their domineering ways when they hear these Magic Words: "I Like to Dance, but Can't We Take Turns Leading?" If someone says them to Bernie, he might finally learn that in dealing, as in dancing, grace lies in knowing it takes two to lead.

Magic Words

UNIVERSAL

82

HANDLE WITH FLAIR

Most of the things we do day in and day out are pretty routine. Shopping, going to the cleaners, putting gas in the car. Simple and fairly dull. But they have to be done. We also have similar chores in the workplace. A large percentage of our time is spent doing these unexciting but necessary chores. But that doesn't mean that we can't bring a little something extra to them. We call this "handling with flair."

For instance, we have a buddy named Paul who mows his lawn once a week. He has a pretty large backyard, so when you throw in raking and weeding the flower beds, he's got a solid hour of work to do. It's not something he looks forward to, so he decided to learn something while he did it. He went out and bought the audiotapes to Gibbon's *Decline and Fall of the Roman Empire*. Unabridged, of course. He figures it will take him two years (throwing in snow shoveling) to listen to the entire work. Gibbon has made him look forward to mowing the lawn.

Peggy, a friend of a friend, always keeps a roll of quarters in the glove compartment of her car. They're for parking meters. But if she sees someone else's parking meter about to go into violation mode, she pops a few quarters in. Once in a while the people she's saving from getting a ticket see her putting the money in. Their gratitude makes it clear how rarely they receive such kindness from a stranger. It makes Peggy feel good. And at a cost of fifty cents you have to agree it's a pretty cheap way to elevate your mood.

Arthur, who's married to Peggy, drives three other people to work every weekday. When there's heavy traffic, and there usually is, the ride takes over an hour. To make the ride more enjoyable, Arthur uses part of his weekend to make up tapes of the music everyone likes. His passengers' tastes range from blues to chamber music, from opera (Arthur's favorite) to folk. Not only do they all enjoy the ride more, they've all learned to appreciate music they weren't familiar with before.

We all have places in our daily routines where we could add some zest, fun, and novelty by handling things with a bit of flair. For instance, send someone you care for flowers, not on their birthday but rather to celebrate the day they graduated from kindergarten (this takes a little research!). You have the brush and the palette. To add color to the canvas of life, all you have to do is PAINT.

83

YOU CAN'T RUN THE RACE UNLESS
YOU SEE THE FINISH LINE

These Magic Words can get you through the grueling hours of a marathon, but they're even more helpful when you're faced with a personal struggle that dominates your day-to-day life.

After graduating from law school, a friend's daughter, Helena, used them to keep up her spirits while she studied for the bar exam. "That exam is so important, and while I was in law school, we loved to scare each other with stories of people we'd heard about—smart people—who'd failed, sometimes twice. By the time I started preparing for the bar, I was convinced I'd be one of the failures. My confidence was gone. Then I decided that unless I changed my attitude I probably would fail. Every day, before I'd settle down to my books, I'd call up an image of myself being sworn in by the judge. I decided who I'd ask to be my sponsor, and I put her in the picture too. I even planned what I'd wear.

"It made all the difference. Once I started seeing my success instead of the ordeal I'd face to achieve it, I breezed right through."

The Magic Words helped another friend of ours too, though Toby would never say that she breezed right through her ordeal. Toby, who runs her own public relations business, got through a major health crisis by focusing not on the difficult treatments she had to undergo, but on the results she'd been told to expect.

It started, she said, when she began to get headaches. "These were not the usual 'take two Tylenol' headaches that most of us get every once in a while. These were more like having your head put in a vise and having Arnold Schwarzenegger apply the pressure. When they didn't go away, I went to my doctor, who put me through a battery of tests. A few days later I went in to see him. I could tell immediately that the news he had to give me was not great. I won't give you the technical rundown, but I had a big problem. Did I have a chance? Yes. Did I have a battle on my hands? You bet I did.

"In the blink of an eye I went from being a normal, fairly happy person, to being a member of that large, silent segment of our population that the healthy seldom think about: patients. To start with, there would be an operation—a main-event type of operation that would take hours. Intensive care for days afterward.

"Then there would be months of grueling treatment. Was the process scary? Damn right it was. Was it tough to go through? You know the answer to that, too. But what helped me is that I refused to focus on the process. I thought only about the result. For me the finish line would be a return to good health. I saw myself on the other side of that line, a healthy Toby, standing there cheering me on for having completed the race. Most of the crises I find myself in now are minor compared to that—problems at work, difficulties with my son, who's a terrible teen—but I still use those Magic Words to urge myself on to the finish."

In the old days of romance movies, we knew that although Hollywood might wreak havoc on our heroine, by the time the closing credits rolled, she'd be living happily ever after. "You Can't Run the Race Unless You See the Finish Line" strengthens us with a vision of our own happy endings.

84

LOOK CLOSELY AT THE FIRST
SYLLABLE OF CONFIDENCE

We have a secret to tell you: confident people aren't confident all the time. In fact, there are plenty of times when their confidence is as thin as a supermodel's wrist. If someone is confident all the time, there's something wrong somewhere.

Betty, a very old friend of ours, is a partner at a top law firm in Washington, D.C. Her resume looks like it was written by her mother: graduated with honors from the University of Michigan; Harvard Law School (edited the law review, too); on the board of directors at three Fortune 500 companies; happily married for twelve years, with two boys (fortunately they're twins so she didn't have to take extra time off!). Whenever we want advice from someone who is confident and self-assured we automatically go to Betty. So when she told us this, it took us aback (to put it mildly).

"In my legal practice I've represented everyone from CEOs to governments, from refugees fleeing totalitarian states to professional baseball players. As a director of several large corporations I've been involved in multibillion-dollar acquisitions and hostile takeovers. Have I been confident in all of these situations? You must be joking. But since I know that it's critically important for my clients and colleagues to have complete trust in me, I make a point of always showing an aura of cool confidence during a difficult situation. "Con" is the first syllable of confidence, right? Well, there's a lot of con in confidence, and though I don't have the abilities that Newman and Redford demonstrated in *The Sting*, I do have enough in me to get past the first few hurdles in a tough situation. I always do my homework, which helps. I weigh the facts and study the problem as intently as a diamond-cutter studies a rare diamond. Then I use a little 'con' to buoy myself and the others who are involved with me. Is it dishonest? No way! We all have doubts from time to time. What's to be gained by sharing them like potato chips at a picnic? I never tell anyone I'm working with that sometimes I go weak in the knees for fear a project won't work. If you find yourself in a lifeboat in the middle of the sea, would you want to sit next to someone who said you might drown? Sit next to me, and I'll tell you we're sure to be rescued, but we have to conserve our food and take turns scanning the horizon."

Note that when Betty talks about conning her clients, she's talking about making them feel confident, not about taking advantage of them by failing to be prepared. That's the kind of con we can live with, and we like these Magic Words because they remind us how important it is to project an image of assurance.

Some people believe that you have to be a hardheaded realist at all times, but as long as you *know* you're playing the grifter's game, the occasional con can give you confidence and inspire those around you.

85

THE 60 PERCENT SOLUTION

These Magic Words are one of the secrets to making a marriage work. The story of Mary and Gerald came from one of our closest friends.

Mary was eight and Gerald was nine when he challenged her to a nail-hammering contest. They lived in Red Oak, Iowa, where Mary's father ran a substantial cattle farm and Gerald's dad was the indispensable town blacksmith. Mary hammered her way to victory, and Gerald fell in love. They were inseparable from that minute on, becoming high school sweethearts. Mary followed Gerald to Drake, where he was an All-American football player. In Mary's senior year, they finally married.

Physically, Gerald and Mary were opposites, he a large strapping fellow with an easygoing manner; she a tiny woman, just five feet tall, who had occasional bursts of temper that reminded Gerald of the top sergeant in his old infantry regiment. But they got along, though like all marriages, theirs had its good and not-so-good days.

On a sunny June weekend, their son Dennis, who lived in New York, flew out to Orange County to celebrate his parents' fiftieth wedding anniversary. It was a big, happy event with friends and family gathering from all over the country to wish Mary and Gerald well. The night before the festivities, Dennis was in the kitchen helping his mother with the dishes. Dennis, whose first marriage had ended in divorce, was thinking of marrying again. He asked his mother what had made her marriage work so well. "Your ability to hammer?" he asked jokingly, recalling the oft-told story of that long-ago contest.

Mary thought for a moment. "I guess it's because we chose the 60 percent solution."

"And what exactly does that mean?" asked John.

"Oh, it's what my mother told me when Dad and I got married. Most people say, 'You've got to share equally,' or 'shoulder half the burden.' That's not what my mother said. She said that if both parties start out with the idea of giving 60 percent to the marriage, you've got a much better chance of succeeding. That adds up to over 100 percent, so the odds are pretty good that things will work out.'

"Hey, Mom," said John, teasing her, "I bet that most of the time you were the one giving the 60 percent. Pop could be pretty lazy."

"If your father hadn't put 60 percent into the marriage, we wouldn't have made it—and you certainly wouldn't be here asking such nosy questions."

As soon as we heard about the 60 percent solution we started to use it in our own lives. Sometimes we'd say the Magic Words aloud to remind our mates they weren't pulling their weight. Sometimes we'd say it to ourselves so we wouldn't forget that life isn't fifty-fifty, and that sometimes one party has to pay a little extra into the marriage account. During the best of times, these Magic Words can get each partner to give a little extra. At all times, "The 60 Percent Solution" is a guarantee that neither spouse will ever overdraw.

86

THERE ARE SOME BOXES YOU
SHOULD JUST NOT OPEN

We're not talking about a misdelivered package from the San Diego Zoo that contains a cobra. Of course you should not open *that* box. What we're referring to are the boxes that we keep stored deep inside of us. Think of them as the boxes Pandora opened, the ones containing all the evils that plague mankind. One box probably contains "old hurts." Another has a fair number of "bitter disappointments." There's also one for "lost loves." And what would life be without "missed opportunities"? The largest box is marked "stupid decisions." There's a reason these parcels from the past shouldn't be opened. Listen to what Naomi, a former colleague of ours, says on the subject.

"I had a great job as an account supervisor in a midsized advertising agency in San Francisco. I had been there for two years and had already had three promotions. I was just around the corner from being made a VP. And then something happened.

"The man I reported to, Tad, was in line to become the company's CEO. He was a hard-driving, take-no-prisoners kind of guy. He told me that if he got the job, he'd take me along with him. Pretty heady stuff. But Tad demanded absolute allegiance. That meant backing him wholeheartedly in meetings, even if I disagreed with him. I felt funny doing this, but after all he had, in effect, promised me the moon. I made some enemies by supporting Tad, but I felt the payoff would be worth it.

"Then one day I came into the office to find that Tad had been fired. My assistant told me that the head of the company wanted to see me. I was told that I had not shown the proper attitude in my unbridled support of Tad. Like Tad, I was out.

"I don't know how many times I played and replayed my mental tape of that morning. Then I decided that I had to stop. I put that tape into a box and closed it for good. Opening it and reviewing the contents would only bring back the anguish. I had learned my lesson. I didn't need to linger over the pain. That led me to look at all the boxes I had stored up over the years: the breakup of my first marriage; the money I lost in my I.R.A. when I let my dumb cousin handle it; the years of fighting with my mother over countless issues. I realized that I had learned as much as I needed to from what was inside all those boxes. It was time to seal them up and put them away in the attic."

Naomi knew what to do about boxes that contained past troubles: keep them open long enough to inoculate yourself, then put them away. To learn from past mistakes is healthy. To linger over them and worry about your failures is not.

This is one way to think of these Magic Words: when you drive your car, you look through the front windshield so you can see the oncoming traffic. Occasionally it is necessary to glance in the rearview mirror. But if you were silly enough to drive with your eyes glued to the rearview mirror, your car would go off the road. So say to yourself, "There Are Some Boxes You Should Just Not Open," lock them in the attic, stop watching the rearview mirror, and keep your eyes on the road.

87

VIAGRA, UNLIKE NIAGARA (FALLS, THAT IS), IS A TWO-WAY PROPOSITION

Certainly the introduction of Viagra into our sex lives has been mostly positive; the reason we don't say totally positive is that in lots of cases the female partner is just confronted by her lover with the fait accompli. He pops the pill in private. Sort of like when Jack Nicholson bashes in the door with his axe in *The Shining,* and declares, "It's me. Johnny. I'm home!"

When we heard the story that follows, we decided it was the perfect illustration of how often the person giving a surprise enjoys it much more than the person getting it. Planning—whether it's for the immediate future or long range—should be done by both the people involved. An occasional surprise is delightful; constant surprises are frightful. That is the lesson to be learned from the good husband who turned into The Villain of Viagra.

We'll let Janice tell it in her own words:

"When my husband, Paul, came home one day with a wicked smile and a bottle of champagne, I knew that something was up.

" 'Jan,' he said, 'I had my annual physical today.'

" 'How'd it go?'

" 'Oh, everything's fine.'

" 'What's the champagne for?'

" 'I asked the doctor for Viagra. I felt a little silly doing it, just like a kid, but he instantly wrote out a prescription. He says he has lots of patients taking it.'

" 'I imagine you'd like to try it,' I said, giving him my own version of a wicked smile.

"He nodded. 'I took the pill about an hour ago. It really works.' Janice then provided an edited version of the month that followed and the resulting sexual activity that rivaled her honeymoon.

"At first it was great," she concluded. "But I realized I was married to a raging libido. I love having sex with Paul, but it was fast becoming not just the major, but the only focus of the time we spent together. Like chocolate and ice cream, there can be too much of a good thing. One night at dinner (after sex, naturally) I started to tell Paul that we might be developing a bit of a problem with this new wonder drug.

" 'I thought you loved having sex with me, Jan.'

" 'I do. It's just that something seems to be missing.'

" 'What's that?'

" 'Spontaneity, for one thing. Initiating the act together, for another. And then there's the matter of romance. You can't take the stuff like it's M&M's, Paul. You see what I mean?' "

Janice and Paul had no problem after that. Paul learned that though women love surprises, they don't want to be surprised EVERY TIME, even when it comes to good sex.

So although the longer version of these Magic Words will probably have limited use, we found the story an amusing way to illustrate partnership problems that can be solved by using the shorter version: "Two-Way Proposition." Say them whenever you're about to embark on a situation where your partner should be involved in the planning. Don't book the vacation, or buy the car, or accept the promotion that will change both your lives without consulting the other person. They want to be part of all important decisions. If you stop a moment and think about it, so do you.

88

300-SECOND SEX

A while ago, attending a birthday party for a mutual friend, Alexandra met a charming, interesting young woman named Sallie. They hit it off immediately and began having lunch every couple of months. Sallie's mate was Mike, a tall man who wore horn-rimmed glasses, favored pinstriped suits, and looked exactly like the banker he was. At 36, Sallie was raising their two-year-old son Jack and finishing her degree as a nurse practitioner. Over one lunch, the conversation turned to sex.

"If you ask women my age, you'll find that practically no one's having sex. Mike and I used to spend every Sunday in bed. Now he's at his office doing some deal or other, and I'm with Jack and trying to study. Every woman I know complains of the same thing—no time for romance, and no time for doing the delicious deed."

A few weeks later, Sallie and Alexandra met for lunch again, and Sallie said, "You know how I was telling you that everybody's practically sexless these days. I heard a neat trick that you probably know about: 300-second sex."

Alexandra allowed as how she wasn't familiar with it and asked Sallie to explain.

"Here's what this person told me. Basically, 300-second

sex—or even 60-second sex, for that matter—is a quickie. Now I have never liked speedy sex. But I said to Mike the other morning, 'Let's have 300-second sex.' Of course he wanted to know what I was talking about. There's nothing like introducing a new concept, you know!"

Alexandra did know.

"Well, he was *really* turned on by this. The fact that he was so turned on made me even more so. Plus it's the surprise that makes it work. I'd never asked him that before. It was about pure lust, and it was just great!"

"Sounds pretty good to me," Alexandra replied.

"But wait, there's more," Sallie said. "I was told there's another version of 300-second sex."

"How could I not want to hear this?!" Alexandra rejoined.

"Here's what this person told me. For 300 seconds, or for about five minutes, you each agree to do exactly what the other wants. There's no mutual stuff in this approach. One person gives and the other gets. After our 'quickie' we decided that we'd take time to try this out. We've always found it a bit embarrassing to say what we want, so we just use body language. It's pretty amazing what can happen."

Any relationship can go through a sexual slowdown, but if you allow it to slide into shutdown mode, you're bound for trouble. And that's what's happening to many couples who just don't have the same kind of time to spend together that they did when they first fell in love. "300-Second Sex"—both the long and short versions—is a great way to get some new excitement going. Satisfaction guaranteed.

89

A FACT IN TIME SAVES
MORE THAN NINE

Remember Sergeant Joe Friday on *Dragnet?* His famous line was "Just the facts, Ma'am. Just the facts.'" And he was right. We often forget what an incredibly useful strategic weapon a fact can be. In today's world of superhype we often lose track of how important facts are. Here's a situation that we think illustrates the point.

Debbie, who's twenty-eight, is a very talented architect at a large firm in Detroit. It's been a delight to watch her career take off. Recently she was made a senior project manager on a professional football stadium that her firm won the contract to design.

At first, Debbie enjoyed her new responsibilities and the pay they brought her. Then things started to change. Since this was a big job she had to quickly add additional architects and draftsmen to her team. She soon found that not all of them were right for the job. The project was budgeted at over three hundred million, and the client turned out to be very demanding even before the first spadeful of earth was dug. Debbie began to have difficulties meeting the goals that each phase demanded.

"I'm going to tell my boss tomorrow how frustrated I am. I think I want off this project. Things are changing so fast, and the client is resisting me at every turn. I just can't seem to make any headway," she told us when we caught up with her one evening at her parents' home.

As she told us more about what was bothering her, what we really heard were Debbie's emotional reactions. Her frustration came across loud and clear, but it wasn't clear what specifically was causing it. We suspected that Debbie's meeting with her boss was doomed from the start. Having been bosses ourselves, we understood how her boss would react to her situation.

"You know, Debbie," one of us said, "there's just one thing we haven't heard from you about this situation." She looked at us quizzically. "The facts. I think your boss will understand the pressure you're under and your frustrations, but unless you present him with a list of facts that describe both the situation you're in and how you need to change it, you won't get the help from him that you need."

Debbie told us that later that night she sat down and wrote out a list that she headed: FACTS. Then she listed them in order of importance to describe the situation she was in, what she needed to change, and what she had to get in order to do the job. When Debbie met with her boss the next day, she didn't mention the whirlpool of emotions that had seemed about to pull her under. She just consulted her list and explained the facts. It didn't take long for him to effect the changes that transformed Debbie's work situation.

Bosses don't want to know about your aggravation and frustration—they have plenty of their own. But facts are clear statements of information that can be acted upon. Keep them short and to the point and present them in a logical order, and you'll find that "A Fact in Time Saves More Than Nine" can save you from looking emotional or incompetent in front of your boss and also give you the upper hand in any argument with a mate or with friends.

90

PRAISE IS A SHORT WORD
THAT GOES A LONG WAY

Last summer we watched a young boy build a sand castle at the beach. He approached his task with the seriousness of a construction engineer working on a forty-story building. He intently shoveled sand into a small blue pail, carrying pail after pail over to a blanket where a man sat reading a paperback book. After a half hour he had a large heap of sand, which he then laboriously patted into a low, squat edifice. When he was finally satisfied with his work, he went over to the man.

"Look, Dad. Look what I did."

The boy's father carefully studied the heap. He walked around it as if inspecting a work of art.

"Charlie, it's a beaut. You've made a great castle. I think it's the best on the beach."

The boy's smile was as radiant as the sun emerging after a week of rain. His father's praise had made him the happiest boy in the world. As we watched this scene it reminded us of the power of praise. And, sadly, of how little most of us receive as adults.

We thought of a story our friend Marty told us. Marty is a management consultant. He was hired by a start-up Internet company that was going through its intense prelaunch period.

People's tempers were reaching the boiling point, rival factions were clawing and scratching for turf, and, to put it mildly, morale was very low. Toni, a brilliant young woman and a key member of the tech staff, had been working fourteen-hour days, seven days a week. She confided to Marty that she was at the end of her tether. A number of job offers were coming her way, and she was tempted to take one. Marty took her aside and asked if there was anything he could do to keep her at the company.

"I think you've been doing a great job, but I also have noticed that your stress level is approaching Mt. Everest. What can I do to help?"

Before she could answer, Toni broke down into tears. When she pulled herself together, Marty discovered that in addition to the stress of the long hours and the pressure, she hadn't received one word of approval, let alone praise, for her work. Marty immediately went to Toni's boss and told him the situation.

"And while you're at it," he concluded, "a few words of praise for the rest of the staff could only help."

The boss acted immediately on Marty's suggestion. An hour after talking to Toni alone in this office, he called all the employees into the conference room. There on the table was an array of Krispy Kremes and Starbucks coffee. He then proceeded to tell each person how much he appreciated what they had accomplished. From then on he made it a point to praise an employee when a job was well done.

"It was a different place after that," Marty told us. "The boss learned a valuable lesson which he's never forgotten. And, by the way, Toni became a vice president and is still with the company. She's real happy she didn't take another offer."

91

THERE'S ONLY ONE CONDITION
FOR FRIENDSHIP

Glenn and Barry had been best friends since junior high and remained close through adulthood. Glenn was shocked to receive a phone call one morning telling him that Barry, a lawyer, had been arrested at his home by FBI agents and charged with multiple counts of money laundering on behalf of a client he was representing in a drug smuggling case.

"How close a friend? He's executor of my estate *and* the godfather to both of my kids," an angry Glenn told us a few days after Barry's arrest. "From the time we were fourteen, we've been each other's confessor and confidant. He knows things about me that my wife and my brother don't know. I can't believe he'd do this! I thought I knew him, but how close a friend can he be?"

When the judge set bail, Glenn drove into town to visit Barry. "He looked wretched," he told us afterward. "It only took a few minutes before both of us were weeping. To see a friend in so much pain was almost more than I could absorb. After a while I pulled myself together.

"I told him, 'Barry, I just want to say that I'm here for you. If necessary, I'll put another mortgage on our house to get you out of here.'

"Barry broke down. He was clearly ashamed, and he said, 'I really let you down, Glenn. My family, you, everyone. I don't know what to say.'"

Glenn interrupted his story about the visit to say, "Let me back up a bit. I have to give you some background here. I have a personal antipathy toward drugs that's way beyond normal. My sister, whom I loved dearly, died of a drug overdose when she was in college. My parents never recovered from it. Barry helped me through this period. I don't know if I would have made it without his help. He, more than anyone, knows how I feel about drugs and the scum who sell them. I knew that in his legal practice he had represented accused drug traffickers. We never talked about it and I never felt comfortable with it, though in theory I agreed with him that everyone deserves competent legal representation no matter what they're accused of doing.

"I knew the moment that Barry said to me, 'I really let you down, Glenn,' that he was telling me he was guilty. I didn't have to ask him directly, I just knew. And that knowledge devastated me. In a sense I felt betrayed by him. But you know what I did after I left him? I went directly to my bank and took out another mortgage on my house. By the next day we had the money together to get Barry out of jail.

"During this entire awful period, I kept thinking of the Magic Words you once said to me: 'There's Only One Condition for Friendship.' And, of course, that condition is 'unconditional.' You can't have a real friendship without it."

Barry served an eighteen-month sentence and was disbarred. When he was released, Glenn, who owns a successful used car business, gave him a job. He also urged Barry into counseling, and, at Glenn's urging, Barry also spends one night a week answering the phones for a suicide hot line. Barry has told Glenn that many of the callers are hooked on drugs. It's too soon to tell whether Glenn's example has given Barry a moral sense that will guide his future, or whether, having been punished, he's spending a short time showing he's a "good boy." But Glenn loved Barry and felt that he deserved a second chance. Considering the severity of the offense, Glenn shows us what friendship should be: the acknowledgment that an act may be bad, coupled with the conviction that the person who did it may still be good.

Not many friends have to endure what Glenn faced, but both of us have been tested by difficult situations. But whether the test is as daunting as scrambling up a canyon wall or as gentle as a stroll down a flowery slope, you have to give your friend the trust and support you would want yourself.

92

NOT EVERY IMPROVEMENT IS A
MEANINGFUL IMPROVEMENT

Why do we feel we have to improve things all the time? Nose too long? Shorten it. Hair gray? Darken it. Kitchen not as modern as the one next door? Remodel it. Breasts not as big as Madonna's? Well, you've got the idea.

There are some changes that matter and some that use up money and energy better spent on other things. When Alexandra mentioned that someone we both knew, a woman named Sandra, had just hired yet another artist, this time to paint a new mural on her living-room wall, Howard muttered the Magic Words about improvement. Just a week before, Sandra had turned down a plea from one of Howard's colleagues who was raising money to support a theater group that gave free performances in poor neighborhoods.

"Sandra always has the money to improve her living room," Howard said, "but I've never seen her take the time or spend the dime to improve her mind or soul." So although we're not against improving the way you look or the place you live, we believe that if you use these Magic Words, you may pause long enough to consider whether you're just giving in to a passing fancy, and whether you might be better off doing some real "interior decorating"—dressing up the mind and soul.

Some things we've found that decorate the mind:

1) Reading a book that you've read before and really liked. You'll understand even more clearly why you liked it the first time.

2) Buying a copy of a magazine you'd ordinarily never buy. Let's say *Scientific American*. Maybe you won't understand everything you read, but maybe you will—and maybe you'll find a new interest that will light up your life.

3) Going to a poetry reading. Boring? Not anymore they're not, and, believe us, from the inner city to the hinterlands, you'll find poetry readings scheduled every week.

4) Starting a journal. It's a secular confession and a nice way to spend time with a person you sometimes neglect: yourself.

It may be tough to locate that little thing we call the soul, but you don't have to see it to spruce it up. You can:

1) Call the friend you had a fight with. Maybe you won't go back to being best buddies, but it hurts you both to cut off the connection.

2) Read to the blind. Or spend a few hours helping at a soup kitchen.

3) Tell the friend or family member who owes you money that you've torn up the IOU (If you can't afford to do that, what about asking for only a partial repayment?)

4) Give someone who needs it a) a pat on the back, b) a hug, c) a kiss, or d) all of the above.

Because we believe that the relentless drive to "improve" our outer world can sometimes leave us with a diminished inner world, we find these Magic Words make us pause before we plunge. Investing more "capital" in improving what's inside pays its own form of interest, teaching us to savor the constant, small pleasures wherever we find them.

93

IF YOU WEREN'T THERE,
YOU REALLY WEREN'T THERE

The dinner party was for ten people, all friends. Bill had called ahead and said that something had come up at his office and he'd be a little late. When he arrived he quickly finished the glass of wine before him and then poured another. When the conversation wound down for a moment, Bill jumped in.

"I heard something unbelievable just as I was leaving my office. Unbelievable, and also terribly sad."

He now had everyone's attention. All eyes were fixed on Bill.

"I got a call telling me that Norman was arrested."

A chorus of "Oh, no" and "not Norman" echoed through the dining room. Everyone at the dinner knew him. Norman was a friend to everyone there.

"What happened?" someone finally asked.

"I was told it was for sexual assault."

"I can't believe that. . . . Norman couldn't do something like that . . . ," said a few people at the table.

"Well, we all better start believing it. That's the story. Apparently, Norman assaulted their baby-sitter a couple of weeks ago while driving her home."

There was a stunned silence that lasted a long while. Then

the rest of the dinner was spent discussing Norman and Joyce, his wife, and how they'd cope with this terrible situation. Norman was a money manager, and he handled investments for a few people at the table. They didn't talk about it, but those people were thinking about their money. Should they move it away from Norman? What else was he capable of doing? They wondered. Was their money safe with him?

The dinner party ended early, and the guests retreated to their homes. Though Norman was indeed a friend, they did what most normal people would do: they called other friends. The calls all started off the same way: "Did you hear what happened to Norman? You won't believe it."

The next day a few of the friends who were at the dinner party called Norman to commiserate. They were there for him, they told him.

"What the hell are you talking about?" Norman asked.

They didn't want to use the word "arrest," so they mumbled "your problem."

"I still don't know what you mean," he told them.

When they finally got it out, there was a silence at the other end, followed by laughter.

"Where the hell did you hear that?"

And then Norman told them that no, he hadn't been arrested for sexual assault. What had happened was that the baby-sitter's parents had sued Norman and his wife because their daughter had slipped on Norman's front steps and suffered a "serious back injury" that could, the suit alleged, "end her dancing career" (which, of course, had not even begun).

How does something like this get started? We remember a small experiment in perception that we tried in high school. Our teacher arranged all of the kids in our class in a line that circled around the classroom. She then whispered into the ear of the boy who was first in line, "I just bought a green, two-story house with red shutters." She told him to whisper the sentence into the ear of the student next to him, who would then repeat it, and so on. By the time it reached the last one in line it had been transformed into "The teacher's husband has bought four stores that sell red suits!"

It took quite a while for Norman and his wife to get the word out to their various friends that Norman had not been arrested, and Norman did, in fact, lose some clients, though they eventually returned.

The moral of this story is that whenever you hear sec-ondhand negative information about someone, remember to use our Magic Words. Reputations and lives are too important to accept hearsay as fact. "If You Weren't There, You Really Weren't There." It's the litmus test we use all the time.

94

THE DEVIL DOES RENTALS

You may know someone like Trisha. She's 37, smart, toned, and seriously beautiful. Her first marriage was to her high school sweetheart in Oklahoma. He owned a garage, and when he couldn't make the payments on it he lost it. Trisha walked out of her gas-station life into a new one in New York and, since then, has always dated older men. Rich—usually very rich— older men. At 35, she married an extremely wealthy man who'd made a fabulous fortune on Wall Street. He was 76. Swathed in sable, with a car and driver to take her everywhere, and a jet at her beck and call, she became a shopper. From the latest couture fashions in New York and Europe, to the perfect furnishings for her apartment on Park Avenue and her homes in Palm Beach and Easthampton, she bought and bought and bought. She also bought tennis lessons, golf lessons, computer, bridge, backgammon—anything she could to occupy her mind and body. Trisha and her husband wanted a baby, but after all the fertility clinics in the world couldn't help, they decided to give up trying.

About that time Trisha fell deeply in love with her tennis instructor. Ted was 39, and doing well professionally. He had a small business selling lessons and gear and lived in a pleasant house in a neighborhood a few miles from Trisha's mansion. No matter how much in love she was with Ted, Trisha couldn't face leaving her plush life. He was bitter about Trisha's decision and told her, "You don't love your husband. You can't have a child with him. I love you and can provide for you, but it's not enough. Your life is nothing but cars and a plane and some animal-skin coats." Within a year, Ted had met and married someone else. Trisha still can't stop herself from driving past Ted's little house and thinking about what might have been.

Larry, an acquaintance of ours, had a job that made him miserable. He's a brilliant salesman, but his boss was a sadist and a pathological liar. Larry was overqualified for what he did, so his work bored him and was in no way meaningful or satisfying. The pay, however, was terrific, and so were the perks. He had a great expense account and a fancy foreign car and got to go to all sorts of parties and openings in order to sell the fashion products his company produced.

Larry was so miserable he quit that job to join two other guys starting up a small, promising business. He gave up the car, the expense account, and the parties and worked in a cramped space, flew economy class, and stayed in budget motels. The business was fascinating and exciting, but he suddenly left his partners to go back to his old job when his former boss offered him more perks, a higher salary than before, and an even pricier car. His partners were devastated. Their company needed just a couple more years before it would be successful. Larry said he wanted his old life back—just for a few years. Then he'd get another job that would make him happy.

Most of us don't sell our soul to the devil, but like Larry and Trisha, we rent it out. We go into relationships and jobs for the kind of temptation that the devil is very good at— money, sex, material things. The devil never wears a suit off the rack, never sings off key, he's always suave, and his stuff looks too good and too perfect. Deep down, we know when the devil is setting out his lures. Never forget that the devil is a great salesman. Unfortunately, what he gives us is an empty life. The devil can't give us love or fulfillment. He's downright awful on inner happiness and true excitement. If you want the hollow perks in life, sit down and have a drink with him. If you want a life with true meaning, tell him to sell his stuff to someone else. His rentals generally turn out to be long-term deals.

95

ANGER IS ONE LETTER
SHORT OF DANGER

These are very important Magic Words. They're not ours, but those of Eleanor Roosevelt, a very wise woman. How can you argue with her? When anger consumes us, danger is never very far away. It could be emotional or even physical danger that comes in the aftermath of uncontrolled anger.

Jake is a very smart guy who for the first ten years of his business career never achieved what we knew he could because of anger. Well educated, well spoken, and generous, Jake could fly off the handle for the most trivial reasons. Aside from yelling, he was also subject to "pitching mound" anger: Jake threw things. Anything that was close at hand. These missiles were never aimed directly at people, but sometimes uncomfortably near them. Now aside from his problem with anger, Jake is a sweet and considerate guy. But anger overshadows the good qualities in a person. Jake tried a lot of things to bank his internal fire. He went to a therapist, which helped some. He tried meditation and that also helped. But his anger, though diminished, was still there. The anger that lurks in all of us can never be totally controlled or dispelled. In fact, Jake is always looking for anything that can help him keep it further in check. Which is why we told him these Magic Words. One night we visited him in his office and found them gracefully stitched on a throw pillow that rested on his sofa. Jake says the words help him, but managing anger is a full-time job. When he does give way to his anger, he finds it's much better to throw the pillow than the telephone.

Tina, who has an antique store in Greenwich Village and a rather short fuse, has a few rules she follows whenever she feels her anger rising. Her first is to get the hell away from the cause of the anger. Do it politely, she says, but do it quickly.

Her second technique is to think of her favorite *Simpsons* episode—the one where Homer joins a cult. This gets her to chuckling. She swears this works almost all the time.

When she's on the telephone and gets angry, she simply tells the other person that her other line is ringing (she only has one, by the way) and then gently hangs up. Slamming the phone down is an absolute no-no. Then she goes for a walk.

Her last rule is to never, and she means never, get behind the wheel of a car when you're angry. If you're lucky you'll just get a speeding ticket. In fact, Tina tries to stay away from anything mechanical when she gets hot under the collar. Everything, from a can opener to a pencil sharpener, is potentially dangerous when anger has you in its grip.

Some people believe that anger is a form of temporary madness. Maybe that's pushing it too far, but the angry you is not the real you. When you're gripped by anger you'll say things, do things, and wish things that the real you would be appalled by. Time, which provides perspective, is the best cure for anger, which is why it makes sense to walk away, cool down, and get some distance from the situation so that you don't say—or do—something you'll regret.

Anger visits all of us. What we have to aim for is to make the visits both rare and of very short duration.

96

WHEN YOU GET INTO A DOWNWARD SPIRAL, HIT THE GROUND RUNNING

One day a few months ago when our friend Frederick went to start his car nothing happened. He called his garage, waited for the truck to arrive, and watched as the man attached the battery cables. He turned on the ignition again. Nothing. His car was towed to the garage, where he learned that not only did he need a new battery, he also needed a new transmission.

When he got to work (an hour and forty minutes late), he was told that he had to see the CEO. Pronto. Ned, the head of the company, listened impatiently to Frederick's tale of the immobilized automobile, then interrupted to announce that since the company had merged with another firm six months earlier, the work of all departments had been reviewed. It had been decided that Frederick's unit would be moved to Denver.

Now Denver may be a terrific place to live, but Frederick was quite happy in Boston. He, his wife, and their two kids had just moved into a new house the month before. Frederick listed reasons why the division should stay in Boston. Ned listened politely, and then said no.

When Frederick returned to his office, there was a message to call his sister. Their mother had slipped that morning and fallen down the stairs. Result? A broken hip. She was being operated on as they spoke, and though the doctor thought she'd pull through fine, she was going to need help. Financial, for the home care she'd need during her recovery, and personal, to keep her going emotionally until she was back to normal.

When Frederick called his wife, Gina, to tell her what had happened, she got her news in first. The dentist had said their daughter needed braces. That was minor compared to the rest of the morning's events, but it was one more thing to make Frederick feel that he was on a downward spiral and things had spun out of his control.

That evening, Frederick and his wife discussed the situation. Even if he was willing to move to Denver, his wife was adamant about staying put. She was taking courses at Boston University. The children were happy with their friends. His mother needed them.

Frederick fell asleep that night and woke at 3 A.M. with an image of his family on one side of a river, his job on the other. The next morning, his wife dropped him off at the garage, where he put the car repair bill on his credit card. In one day he'd gone from being a man who had responsibilities and the money to pay for them to being one who had only the responsibilities.

By coincidence Howard called him that morning to say he'd be in Boston for the day. Could Frederick have lunch? When Howard learned what had happened, he didn't offer up meaningless words of sympathy. Instead, he said the Magic Words: "When you're in a downward spiral, hit the ground running."

After they'd ordered, Howard prodded Frederick into writing down the names of companies that might hire him. He asked the waiter for a Boston phone directory, and together they made a list of places that could provide home care for invalids. "You're going to get another job," Howard assured him, "but always be prepared for the worst. They want you to move in a month. If you haven't gotten another job by then, go to Denver. The company will pay for a hotel or apartment while, presumably, the family gets ready to move. You fly back weekends to see them and to keep interviewing. And you tell your sister you'll pay more than your share toward your mother's care since she'll be here and you won't."

Frederick called the companies, and he never had to move to Denver at all. Before the month was out he had two job offers, both in Boston and both paying substantially more than he was currently making. The only part of the story that didn't have a happy ending was that his daughter hated her braces.

At times in our lives we all find ourselves in a downward spiral. It's scary being out of control, which is why we need to say, "Hit the Ground Running." They're the Magic Words that put us back in charge and give us a plan for what we'll do when we hit bottom.

97

PUBLIC ENEMY #2

It was a short, formal letter, very carefully composed. The heavy, white stationery appeared to be the kind usually engraved by a fancy store. But the sender had simply typed her name and address and centered it at the top of the page.

Dear Alison Dodd,
[all names used here are fictitious],

I am an advocate of journalism with integrity. It is in that spirit that I felt it my responsibility to write to you about one of your reporters, Louise A _____ .

While I have found her columns on health and fitness at times helpful and interesting, I feel that you, as her superior, should be aware that she is freelancing for one of the companies she often writes about, R_____ . I hope that you find this information useful in maintaining the high standards and integrity of your newspaper.

Very sincerely,

Marcia Smithson

As soon as she received the letter, Alison asked to see Louise in her office. When she came in, Alison showed her the letter.

"I'm stunned," Louise replied. "I can't imagine who hates me enough to write such a poisonous letter. Who would want to ruin my life?"

Since Louise was not an employee of the paper, she was entitled to do additional freelance work. When she was approached by the company mentioned in the letter, Louise had immediately asked her boss, Alison, if it would be okay to do the project, and had gotten the go-ahead so she had nothing to fear in terms of being fired.

As soon as she left her boss's office she started to track down "Marcia Smithson" and found that there was no such person, and no such address as the one the sender gave. The postmark yielded no clues, nor did the phone book.

From the minute she received the letter, Louise speculated on who had sent it. Every friend she'd told about her freelance work was suspect. Trouble was, she had a lot of friends. Doubt and distrust began to poison her mind. For weeks, then months, she was sick at heart that someone she knew well could have done this to her.

At last, after a few years, she stopped thinking about the incident. Then, one morning, a letter came in the mail. It was from an old friend who wrote that she had found God and wanted to cleanse her soul. "Please forgive me for all the pain I've caused you because of my envy," the letter read. "I have lived for years in torment over what I have done and I want to atone for all my sins."

Louise thought the woman had gone completely nuts. She hadn't heard from her in over a decade. Moreover, this woman had never done anything to hurt Louise, so why was she asking forgiveness? A day later it struck—she was the Marcia from that long-ago letter.

Since the FBI has long held the right to designate Public Enemy #1, we'll have to leave that slot to the criminals pictured on the wanted posters. But surely the law enforcement officers won't mind if we designate serious, acute envy as Public Enemy #2.

Envy is as poisonous and corrosive as acid, eating away at a person, a relationship, or a nation. It can ruin lives—and it has. Envy has a physical component. You can actually feel it in your body—it's that twitch you get in your gut, the wrench in your chest. When envy enters your world, seeping into your pores, you're allowing the enemy to take over. Say the Magic Words "Public Enemy #2" to help you slap the evil monster on a wanted poster, round it up, and send it to jail. You'll feel a whole lot better.

98

EGO SNACKS

We have a mutual friend who is movie-star handsome with loads of charisma, a bestselling author and professional athlete who graduated from an Ivy League school. Women come on to this man all the time. Although by his own admission he's been tempted, he's been monogamous for over fifteen years. Communication between him and his wife is great, and she laughs at his tales of the more aggressive female fans he encounters at book readings and after TV appearances. But it's not just the communication that makes their relationship so solid. It's the ego snacks they feed each other.

A while back, we mentioned the "hungry ego" theory put forward by well-known psychiatrist Dr. John Train. Each one of us has an ego that needs satisfaction and fulfillment. Ego snacks are a handy form of emotional nourishment that costs you absolutely nothing to give to yourself or to someone else. And the effects can be amazing. The athlete's wife, for example, tells him—often—that he's the sexiest man in the world. Sounds like a simple thing to say, doesn't it? But how many women let their men know how sexy and smart they are after ten—or even five—years of living together? Those are the kinds of words that plump up his ego—and one of the reasons the athlete doesn't stray.

You may protest that ego snacks are just a form of flattery. There's a big difference between the two. Flattery is usually insincere and overdone; for an ego snack to work, it must be genuine—you must mean what you say. The athlete's wife does indeed find him the sexiest man alive, and when she says it, he knows she truly believes it.

What if no one's feeding your ego? You consider yourself a pretty solid citizen, you consider your self-esteem level to be healthy, but there are times when you—like the rest of us—feel a little empty, a bit lonely or melancholy. Check out your ego. Has it been nurtured lately? Has anyone praised you for doing fine work, or being a good mother or father? Has anyone told you, "You look great!"?

We all need ego nutrition to keep our self-esteem and sense of worth in good shape. If you're feeling deprived or blue, give yourself an ego snack. Remind yourself of how disciplined you are when you drag yourself out for your daily early-morning run. Recap what you've achieved over the past six months. Summarize your good points, how generous you are, what a good friend you have been, how brilliantly you tamed your computer . . .

Every day newspapers, magazines—and friends—report layoffs and downsizing. When someone loses a job, the ego takes a big beating. People who've been let go feel they aren't as smart as they thought they were, that they'll never get a job again or will have to settle for something way below what they're worth. Tough moments like these bruise the ego and call for repair work. When people you know are going through a rough patch, it's nice to cheer them up with a lunch date or dinner, but don't forget to provide at least one course for those starving egos.

And don't forget a snack for yourself: You have a big birthday coming up and you're looking pretty good; some of the things you said at a cocktail party were pretty clever; you made a few sharp moves at the office; you've brought up a couple of wonderful kids—give yourself credit where credit is due. Keep a few ego snacks like these in your back pocket and munch on them daily for best results.

99

THE CLEAN SLATE CLUB

Marge and Paula met and bonded on a long flight from Los Angeles to Boston. They were from the same suburban town north of the city, had both been visiting family, shared many of the same interests, and were both on the lookout for career opportunities. Marge's last child was in school full-time, and she wanted to return to work. Paula had recently been downsized from her job. As they flew eastward, they talked about their dreams of owning a business and never having to report to a boss who screamed or was indecisive, of buying a second home on the Cape, salting away a comfortable nest egg for the future—and having some fun and good times while earning a living.

They made a lunch date as the plane was landing and met many times over the next few weeks as they hatched a plan to start up a small business they hoped would soon grow into a big one. Paula was to be the head of operations, Marge would be the creative director. Their first move would be to open a store that sold children's clothes and toys, and they'd expand the franchise as quickly as they could. Their intensely close friendship flourished as they worked day and night to launch their business.

The doors to their boutique opened six months later. That's when the troubles began. A small conglomerate wanted to buy the store. Marge wanted to keep it going. Paula felt they should make a deal and make some money. There were disagreements, then open fights, then threats of litigation. The friendship—and the partnership—degenerated to the point where they closed the store and went their separate ways.

A few months after the acrimonious separation, Marge called Paula and said she'd gone over and over what had happened.

"We made some good and bad decisions," she told Paula, "and we really didn't know each other well enough to be in business together."

"I've been thinking the same thing," Paula said, "and I really miss you. If there is any way we could be friends again—NO business involved—"

"That's why I'm calling. We closed the store, so the issues between us have been resolved. If we could wipe the slate clean and start all over again as buddies—"

They did just that. Wiped out their wrangling over glasses of Amstel light and pizza. Vowed over sips of espresso that they would never allude to the painful past. And the friendship was back on track and continues to thrive.

Wiping the slate clean usually involves two people who have been locked in an ongoing dispute or who have argued bitterly in the past. These kinds of disagreements can happen in a family, business, friendship, or marriage. Wiping the slate clean does not mean sweeping unresolved concerns under the carpet, where resentment can spread as fast as fleas and come back to bite you at another time. It does not refer to a situation where a wife says to her husband (or vice versa), "Since we can't resolve this issue, let's just the wipe the slate clean and start all over again." "Issues" usually don't go away unless they are dealt with.

To belong to the Clean Slate Club, the parties have to submit to the initiation process. They must agree that the issues between them have been resolved—that they *won't* refer to what's happened or dip into the past and dredge up ill will, and that they *will* start fresh and carry no baggage.

Wiping the slate clean gives us a chance to make a new start and to change old, ingrained habits and patterns. When you've made too many marks on the blackboard, it becomes a confusing mess. Always keep an eraser nearby—it's one of the handiest tools you'll ever own.

100

CONNECT-CONNECT

Alexandra's air conditioner dies so regularly that she and Kathy, the dispatcher at the repair service, have become phone buddies. One morning when she called to finally have a new unit installed, she and Kathy got to chitchatting.

"What are you up to now?" Kathy wanted to know.

Alexandra explained she was writing this book and asked Kathy if she had any Magic Words to offer.

"Connect-connect," the dispatcher replied immediately.

"What does that mean?"

"My husband and I have been married thirty-five years, and we've known each other since grade school. We got married right after high school and have had the usual ups and downs. But I can tell you the reason that we're 100 percent solid is that we talk everything through."

"I'm always hearing that men 'don't like to talk,' " Alexandra responded. "Your husband must be a different breed."

"Listen, a lot of women don't like to communicate about what's important to them either. He's a guy like any other, but we realized early on that the only way we were going to make it was to connect with each other all the time. And I'm here to tell you it's worked. You have to connect on both sides. That's why I call it connect-connect."

Communication is at the center of all our lives. Whether we realize it or not we're communicating all the time. Sometimes we don't use words. We wave to hail a cab. The catcher on a baseball team flashes signs to the pitcher. Most of the time, however, we use words. When they fail us, we're in trouble. How many marriages wind up on the rocks because of a "failure to communicate"? Plenty. Communication is not dependent on a good vocabulary. If only it were.

There's hardly a day when we don't run into roadblocks that prevent us from communicating something to someone who's important in our lives. What are some of these roadblocks?

Anger usually has a starring role when a connection fails. Not knowing what's really on our minds is another. Embarrassment and laziness come into play too. And there are a lot of folks who simply don't know how to talk to each other. People often believe they're communicating when they're simply spouting words. It's not a matter of talking "to" or "at" another person, it's about talking "with." In other words making a connection. A big part is simply listening. Listening hard. Making no judgments. Not interrupting. Sometimes this is really difficult to do. This kind of serious listening and honest talking is what connect-connect is all about.

101

TIME IS HONEY

These words are perfect for the stressed-out times we live in. We say them to ourselves almost every day.

Since we were kids we've all heard the phrase "Time is money." In fact, a lot of us have had it hammered into us. Certainly, if you work for an hourly wage (and this includes everyone from steelworkers to psychoanalysts), time is money. You don't get paid unless you put the time in. But time is a lot of other things. Time that's reserved for ourselves, whether it's to stretch out in a hammock or learn a foreign language, is as important to our health as sleep.

We all look forward to our vacations. Whether it's a fishing trip or a visit to the Grand Canyon, our yearly holidays take us back to the time when we were kids. But the summers that once seemed endless are now condensed into one or two weeks. That's why these Magic Words are so important. There is honeyed time in every day, if we see it and take it. Think of it as a wide-awake catnap, something short, and refreshingly sweet, that is there just for you.

Ginger, who works as an account executive in an advertising agency, has a very busy schedule. She travels frequently, and when a problem arises—which is often—she might not make it home until eight. Her husband, Bruno, owns a restaurant where he's also the chef. His hours are even longer than Ginger's. He leaves the house before 6 A.M. and frequently comes home when she is already asleep.

Obviously, the time they spend together is precious. Early on they figured out that until things changed and they both had more time, their free moments would be spent together: honey time. Luckily, they both like to garden. And play tennis. But the time they look forward to most is the time they spend reading to each other. Ginger and Bruno both draw up lists of four books they really want to read, then they exchange lists. Each selects one book from the other's list. That way both of them are pretty sure of enjoying the books they're reading together. And since the outside world is always ready to intrude, whenever they read to each other, they turn the phone off. Telemarketers should be shut out of your life when you're luxuriating in a pool of time that is truly your own.

Here are some things we like to do when we have "honey time":

1) Take a walk without a set destination—if you have a dog, let him (or her) take *you* for a walk.

2) Let your mind wander. Daydreams can sweeten life.

3) Have a glass of lemonade. Most importantly, MAKE the lemonade and take your time doing it.

4) Read a book that you read in college and missed the

beauty of completely because you stayed up all night to finish it.

5) Don't call up that old friend you haven't spoken to in months—write a letter! Snail mail, not e-mail.

6) Most importantly, forget the TICK TOCK TICK TOCK of time. Just lie back and taste its sweetness.

AFTERWORD

Writing this book has truly been a journey for us. It's taken us through a landscape of emotions that ranged from sorrow to joy. We hope these Magic Words that have been so much a part of our life will become part of yours, too. Pick out the ones that apply to you and tuck them in a handy mental cabinet for quick use when the time is right. You wouldn't set out on a long trip without a spare tire in your trunk, so have a few Magic Words always ready for the unexpected turns life brings all of us.

As you now know, many of these Magic Words have been passed on to us. We'd love to know what Magic Words you use. Just send them to us at www.ourmagicwords.com. Remember, you can never have too many Magic Words.

HOWARD AND ALEXANDRA

© MARA BODIS-WOLLNER

ABOUT THE AUTHORS

HOWARD KAMINSKY was the president and publisher of three major publishing houses: Warner Books, Random House, and William Morrow/Avon. Also the author of several screenplays, four novels (cowritten with his wife, Susan), and numerous magazine articles, he lives in New York City and Connecticut.

ALEXANDRA PENNEY's four bestsellers include the mega-hit *How to Make Love to a Man*. In addition to serving as editor in chief of *Self* magazine, she has written lifestyle columns for the *New York Times Magazine* and contributed regularly to numerous others. Currently launching a national magazine for women, she lives in New York City.